History of the Jews

An Enthralling Guide from Ancient Times to the Present

© **Copyright 2023 - All rights reserved.**

The content contained within this book may not be reproduced, duplicated, or transmitted without direct written permission from the author or the publisher.

Under no circumstances will any blame or legal responsibility be held against the publisher, or author, for any damages, reparation, or monetary loss due to the information contained within this book, either directly or indirectly.

Legal Notice:

This book is copyright protected. It is only for personal use. You cannot amend, distribute, sell, use, quote, or paraphrase any part, or the content within this book, without the consent of the author or publisher.

Disclaimer Notice:

Please note the information contained within this document is for educational and entertainment purposes only. All effort has been executed to present accurate, up-to-date, reliable, and complete information. No warranties of any kind are declared or implied. Readers acknowledge that the author is not engaging in the rendering of legal, financial, medical, or professional advice. The content within this book has been derived from various sources. Please consult a licensed professional before attempting any techniques outlined in this book.

By reading this document, the reader agrees that under no circumstances is the author responsible for any losses, direct or indirect, that are incurred as a result of the use of the information contained within this document, including, but not limited to, errors, omissions, or inaccuracies.

Free limited time bonus

Stop for a moment. We have a free bonus set up for you. The problem is this: we forget 90% of everything that we read after 7 days. Crazy fact, right? Here's the solution: we've created a printable, 1-page pdf summary for this book that you're reading now. All you have to do to get your free pdf summary is to go to the following website:

https://livetolearn.lpages.co/enthrallinghistory/

Once you do, it will be intuitive. Enjoy, and thank you!

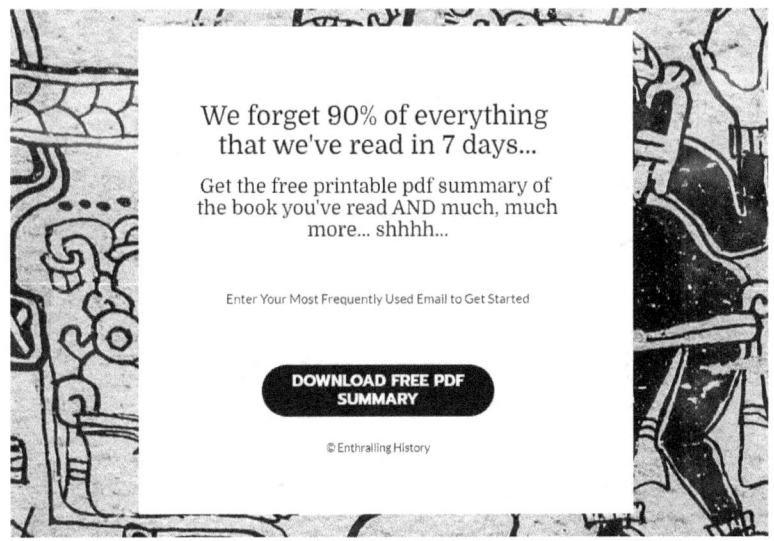

Table of Contents

INTRODUCTION 1
CHAPTER 1: WHAT IS JUDAISM? 3
CHAPTER 2: ANCIENT ISRAEL 13
CHAPTER 3: THE SECOND TEMPLE PERIOD (540 BCE-135 CE) ...24
CHAPTER 4: BYZANTINE JUDAISM (324-640CE) 34
CHAPTER 5: MEDIEVAL JUDAISM I: ISLAM AND THE SPANISH GOLDEN AGE 43
CHAPTER 6: MEDIEVAL JUDAISM II: CRUSADES AND THE MAMLUK PERIOD 52
CHAPTER 7: THE HOLOCAUST 61
CHAPTER 8: MODERN ISRAEL 72
CHAPTER 9: CUSTOMS, TRADITIONS, SYMBOLS, AND ART 83
CHAPTER 10: FAMOUS JEWS: AN ENTHRALLING COLLECTION ...92
CONCLUSION 102
HERE'S ANOTHER BOOK BY ENTHRALLING HISTORY THAT YOU MIGHT LIKE 106
FREE LIMITED TIME BONUS 107
BIBLIOGRAPHY 108

Introduction

The history of the Jews is the story of a people, a nation, and a religion. From a nomadic tribe of seventy people grew a nation that impacted the world on multiple levels. The religion established in the Sinai desert over three millennia ago persists today as Judaism, with about fifteen million followers. The history of the Jews isn't about one country or even one continent. It is global, as more Jews have lived outside Israel than in their ancient homeland for two thousand years. Judaism gave birth to Christianity and influenced Islam; thus, over half of the world's population follows at least some of the teachings of the Jewish Tanakh (Old Testament).

What, exactly, is a Jew? Is being "Jewish" a national identity with a shared history? Is it an ethnic identity with a collective culture? Can one be an atheist and still be a Jew? Can a person follow Judaism but not have an ethnic Jewish background? If one's mother is Jewish, but the father is not, is that person still Jewish? The answer to all these questions is "yes."

It's hard to put "Jewishness" in a box since it is full of schisms, disputes, paradoxes, and evolving history and culture. Yet history, ethnicity, and culture have always connected the Jews. Although many Jews don't go to synagogue or temple, they will gather for the Seder (Passover) meal and attend rites of passage like a bat or bar mitzvah. The Jews have persevered as a minority culture despite attempts to wipe them off the face of the earth. They have adapted to change with "chutzpah," developing ingenuity and innovation.

Today, the State of Israel has close to ten million people, about three-quarters of whom are ethnic Jews, with the rest primarily Arab Palestinians. Almost fifteen million Jews of the diaspora live in the United States, France, Canada, and elsewhere in the world. The Jews have contributed remarkably to the cultures of the lands where they lived and have changed the course of world history. Understanding the history of the Jews is essential to deciphering world history in general and the current political scene in the Middle East.

From the era of the patriarchs to the present day, Jewish history covers almost four thousand years and encircles the earth. This book endeavors to guide readers through the thousands of years of Jewish history, from the Jews' time as nomadic herders to the present day. It explores the patriarchs, the exodus from Egypt, the kingdom of Israel, and its fall. It traces Jewish history through the reign of the Macedonians, the Romans, the Byzantines, and the Islamic caliphates. It will explain why most Jews left their homeland to spread throughout the earth and why many returned in the past two centuries. It will unpack the horrors of the Holocaust and why and how the modern State of Israel was established.

The Jews have always believed that history has a purpose, a belief that has enabled them to maintain dignity and tenacity through unimaginable struggles and persecution. From their history's inception, their religion informed them that "all the families of the earth shall be blessed in you."[1] Let's travel back to ancient Mesopotamia and uncover the history of the enthralling Jewish people.

---

[1] Bereshit (Genesis) 12:3, Torah, *The Complete Tanakh: The Jewish Bible with a Modern English Translation and Rashi's Commentary.*
https://www.chabad.org/library/bible_cdo/aid/63255/jewish/The-Bible-with-Rashi.htm

Chapter 1: What Is Judaism?

Judaism, the religion of the Jewish people, is monotheistic, worshiping only one deity who introduced himself as לִיהוָה (YHVH) or אֱלֹהֵיכֶם: (Elohim). Many Jews believe writing out the names of their deity is disrespectful, so they write it as G-d in English. They base this practice on the book of Devarim (Deuteronomy), which says they shouldn't desecrate, destroy, or erase the name of G-d or anything to do with him.[2] If they write out G-d's name and the document is deleted or destroyed, then G-d's name is erased.

Judaism's scripture is the Tanakh, which has the same material as the Old Testament in the Christian Bible (minus the Apocrypha). However, it only has twenty-four books rather than thirty-nine. Samuel, Chronicles, and Kings are each one book instead of two, and all the minor prophets form one book. The Tanakh has three sections: Torah, Nevi'im, and Ketuvim.

The Torah is the five books of Moses (the first five books of the Old Testament). Historically, Jews considered the entire Tanakh divine, yet they reverenced the Torah most highly because their scriptures say the whole nation witnessed its transmission. Moses received it on Mount Sinai while millions of Israelites stood trembling below as the ram's horn blasted, smoke enveloped the mountain, thunder roared, and lightning flashed.[3] The Torah contains the Jewish accounts of the beginning of life,

---

[2] Devarim (Deuteronomy) 12:2-4, Torah, *Tanakh*.

the birth of the Israelite nation, and the laws given by G-d for them to follow.

When all five books of the Torah are handwritten by a specially-trained scribe on a single parchment scroll, this is called *Sefer Torah*. This precious and sacred scroll is kept in a special ornamental chamber in the synagogue called the Torah Ark. It is read in Hebrew using cantillation, a kind of chanting, on Shabbat (the Sabbath), at Monday and Thursday morning prayers, and on special holy days.

The next section of the Tanakh, the Nevi'im, contains the writings of the prophets. However, the books of Eichah (Lamentations) and Daniel are included in the Ketuvim. Some earlier Israelite history is also in the Nevi'im: Yehoshua (Joshua), Shoftim (Judges), Shmuel (Samuel), and Melachim (Kings). The Ketuvim (Writings) has poetic books, such as Tehillim (Psalms) and Mishlei (Proverbs), and historical accounts, such as Ruth and Queen Esther.

Another influential book for Judaism is the Talmud, which contains teachings by rabbis (religious leaders) on Jewish theology and history throughout the years. The Talmud includes the Mishna: oral laws and interpretations of the Torah's laws, completed in written form in the 3rd century of the Common Era. The Talmud's other section is the Gemara, a collection of commentaries by rabbis.

How do today's Jews view Judaism's scriptures? It depends on which sect they follow. The Orthodox Jews believe G-d literally dictated the Torah to Moses, and they do not question that its stories are true and its laws should be followed. They passionately believe in a Messiah who will come from the lineage of King David and usher in an age of righteousness, peace, and justice. They believe G-d will resurrect the dead and create a new heaven and earth.

The Orthodox Jews concur with Rabbi Moses ben Maimon (1134-1204 CE), who wrote the *Mishneh Torah*, a codification of Jewish law from the Torah and Talmud. He said, "I believe with perfect faith that the entire Torah that is now in our possession is the same that was given to Moses, our teacher, peace be upon him."[4]

---

[4] Eli Cohn-Wein, "The Golden Age of Jewish Philosophy," *Sefaria*. https://www.sefaria.org/sheets/327268?lang=bi

Rabbi Moses ben Maimon (Rashi)
https://commons.wikimedia.org/wiki/File:Maimonides-2.jpg

Orthodox Judaism has two sub-groups: the ultra-conservative Haredim (9 percent of Israel's Jewish population) and the Datiim (13 percent of Israel's Jews). Haredi means "trembling," and these Jews are highly devout. The Hasidic Jews of New York City are a sub-group. Like the Haredim in Israel, they live in separate neighborhoods, socialize mainly among themselves, and wear distinctive clothing. The men usually wear a black coat and hat, and the women wear modest dresses and a head scarf or wig. The Datiim are also theologically conservative but don't separate themselves from mainstream society. The men wear a yarmulke (skullcap), and married women cover their hair.

The second sect is Reformed Judaism, known as Hilonim in Israel, where it is followed by 49 percent of the Jews. In 1837, Abraham Geiger declared, "The Talmud must go, the Bible, that collection of mostly so beautiful and exalted human books, as a divine work must also go."[5]

From that point, Reformed Jews denied the divine origin of the Tanakh, considering it to be the work of men. Shortly after, Rabbi Isaac Mayer Wise declared disbelief in a bodily resurrection or a messiah. He

---

[5] Walter Jacob, ed., *The Pittsburgh Platform in Retrospect: The Changing World of Reform Judaism* (Pittsburgh: Rodef Shalom Congregation Press, 1985), 104.

omitted the traditional prayers about returning to Jerusalem to rebuild the temple and eliminated the dietary laws. In 1885, Reformed Jews rejected circumcision as "savage." By 1972, only one in ten Reformed rabbis in the United States believed in G-d in the traditional Jewish sense. They self-identified as agnostic, humanistic, or existentialist.[6] In Israel, 40 percent of the Hilonim Jews do not believe in G-d.

The third sect, Conservative Judaism (known as Masorti in Israel), is the middle ground between the Orthodox and Reformed sects. Conservative Jews were a sub-branch of the Reformed Jews with more moderate ideas of what needed reforming. Zacharias Frankel started with the practices that most Jews had already stopped following, "that the forward progress will seem inconsequential to the average eye."[7]

The Masorti Jews, who make up 29 percent of the Jews in Israel, follow traditional Judaism, believing G-d created the world and made a covenant with the Israelites. They accept the laws of the Torah regarding lifestyle and the Mishnah and Talmudic teachings on the Torah. However, they doubt that G-d literally dictated the Ten Commandments and the rest of the Torah to Moses, although they believe it is a divine teaching of G-d's will. They think they must carefully consider modern science with regard to their religious beliefs. In areas where science and Torah appear to contradict, they interpret religious tradition to comply with scientific facts while recognizing that science is not infallible.

In 1886, Conservative Judaism launched the Jewish Theological Seminary of America in New York City. The seminary permitted driving cars to Shabbat services, previously forbidden because the car's engine "lit a fire," which the Torah forbids on the Sabbath. Actually, the Torah forbids lighting a cooking fire inside the house on the day of rest, and somehow that got applied to all fires.[8]

Within a century, Conservative Jews in the United States had reached the point where they no longer believed in the divine authorship of the Torah, considering its stories mythical. One offshoot, the "Reconstructionists," completely abandoned belief in the supernatural.

---

[6] Theodore I. Lenin, et al. *Associates, Rabbi and Synagogue in Reform Judaism* (West Harford: Central Conference of American Rabbis, 1972) 98-99.

[7] Michael A. Meyer, *Response to Modernity: A History of the Reform Movement in Judaism* (New York: Oxford University Press, 1988), 85.

[8] Shemot (Exodus) 35:3, Torah, *Tanakh*.

Another spin-off, the Institute for Traditional Judaism, believes Moses did receive the Torah from G-d at Mount Sinai, but the scrolls were lost during the Babylonian exile and the temple's destruction. This group believes the Torah we have today is a 6th-century BCE reconstruction of what the Jews of that time considered the original manuscripts.

One thing is clear: Judaism revolves around the Torah, although Jews interpret it differently. Some take it literally, some say it is allegorical, and some say myth. What is in the Torah? This chapter will explore the book of Bereshit (Genesis), and chapter two will review the rest of the Torah. Bereshit tells of creation, the first sin, and the great flood. It introduces the patriarchs who fathered the Israelite tribe, the ancestors of the Jews.

The Torah begins with creation. G-d created day and night and separated the earth's waters from the water in the atmosphere. He formed dry land and plant life. He made the sun to rule the day, the moon to rule the night, and the stars and planets to shed light on the earth. Next, G-d created sea creatures and winged animals. After this, G-d made the animals that walked and crawled on the earth. G-d's final act was creating human beings in his image, male and female. G-d ceased the work of creation on the seventh day, which he made a holy day of rest for human beings.[9]

The Torah account of creation differs markedly from other Mesopotamian origin stories, such as the *Enuma Elish*. In the macabre Babylonian myth, the creator god Apsu and his wife Tiamat, the deity of chaos, created the younger gods. To their annoyance, the young gods kept them awake night and day with riotous singing and dancing, so Apsu decided to destroy them. But the young god Enki launched a pre-emptive strike, killing Apsu. Then Tiamat sent eleven hideous demons to slaughter the young gods. However, Enki's son Marduk conjured up his hurricane powers, blew up his grandmother's body, fileted her like a fish, and created the sky and the earth with the two halves of her body.[10]

The Torah says that G-d planted the Garden of Eden for Adam and Eve, with the Tree of Life and the Tree of Knowledge of Good and Evil standing in the middle. G-d told Adam they could freely eat from any

---

[9] Bereshit (Genesis) 1-2, Torah, *Tanakh*.

[10] *Enuma Elish: The Seven Tablets of Creation*, trans. Leonard William King (London: Luzac, 1902). https://www.sacred-texts.com/ane/enuma.htm

tree except the Tree of Knowledge. But the serpent tempted Eve, telling her that if she ate from the Tree of Knowledge, she would be like the angels, knowing good and evil. Eve ate the fruit and gave it to her husband, who was with her, and he also ate it.

After eating the forbidden fruit, Adam and Eve lost their innocence. G-d cursed the serpent, telling him Eve's descendant would crush his head, although the serpent would bite his heel. He exiled Adam and Eve from the garden lest they eat from the Tree of Life and live forever. From then on, the earth was cursed, work was hard, childbearing was painful, and immortality was lost.[11]

A mural of the serpent in Eden, painted by Chaim ben Yitzchak ha-Levi Segal in the Cold Synagogue in Mogilev, Lithuania (now Belarus) in the 1740s. Belarus authorities destroyed the synagogue in 1938, and this photo and others taken by El Lissitzky are all that remain.
https://commons.wikimedia.org/wiki/File:Cold_synagogue_in_Mogilev_The_Garden_of_Eden_Serpent_by_El_Lissitzky.jpg

Adam and Eve's first son Cain killed his brother Abel, and each generation became increasingly violent and corrupt. G-d decided to blot out human life, but Noah found favor in G-d's eyes. He told Noah to build an ark and bring his family on board, with one pair of all the animals and enough food for the people and animals to eat. Noah was to bring seven pairs of "clean" (sacrificial) animals on the ark. At this point,

---

[11] Bereshit (Genesis) 2:8-3:24.

humans and animals were vegetarian.[12] Noah and his sons built the ark, and the heavens opened. It rained for forty days, and the flood waters rose until they covered the mountains.

After the waters subsided, the ark rested on the mountains of Ararat, on the border between present-day Turkey and Armenia. After his family and the animals left the ark, Noah built an altar and sacrificed some of the clean animals. G-d gave the rainbow as a covenant that he would never again destroy the earth with a flood and permitted humans and some animals to become carnivorous.[13]

The Torah's flood account resembles the Sumerian *Eridu Genesis* and the Akkadian *Epic of Atrahasis*. In the Sumerian and Akkadian versions, the gods were angry at humans and decided to destroy them with a flood, but Enki warned a priest to build an ark and take the animals on it. The ancient Greeks, Chinese, Aztecs, and multiple civilizations worldwide had a similar flood story.

After the flood, the Torah says humans spread out over the earth, and one Semitic family from the lineage of Noah's son Shem settled in the city of Ur in southern Sumer (Iraq). Today, the ruins of Ur sit in a desert wasteland, but in ancient times, it was an incredibly wealthy city close to where the Euphrates River emptied into the Persian Gulf. Global cooling lowered the Gulf levels, and silt from the Euphrates and Tigris rivers moved the Gulf's shoreline about thirty miles away.

The father of this Semitic family in Ur was Terah. Like the Sumerians, he worshiped multiple gods.[14] For some reason, perhaps due to climate change, Terah packed up his family and herds of sheep, goats, and camels and followed the Euphrates north into today's Turkey. They settled in Haran near the border of today's Syria.

G-d called Terah's son Abram to leave his father's house and go to a new land when he was seventy-five years old. G-d told Abram he would make him into a great nation. He would bless Abram, and all the families of the earth would be blessed in Abram. Abram traveled south into the land of Canaan, which G-d said he would give to his descendants. That was problematic, as Abram had no children because his wife Sarai could not conceive. But G-d promised his descendants

---

[12] Bereshit (Genesis) 1:29-30.
[13] Bereshit (Genesis) 6-9.
[14] Yehoshua (Joshua) 24:2, Nevi'im, *Tanakh*.

would be as uncountable as the stars in the sky.

When Abram was ninety-nine years old, G-d changed his name to Abraham (father of a multitude) and Sarai's name to Sarah (princess). Despite Sarah being ninety and infertile even when young, G-d made a covenant that Abraham and Sarah would have a son in one year. Abraham was to be the father of many nations. For his part of the covenant, Abraham and all the males in his camp had to be circumcised. From then on, all baby boys should be circumcised eight days after birth.

As G-d promised, Sarah miraculously conceived and had a baby a year later, when Abraham was one hundred years old. They named him Isaac, meaning laughter. When Isaac was grown, Abraham sent his steward back to Haran, where some of his relatives still lived, to find a wife for Isaac. His steward arrived at the well of Haran with ten camels, extremely nervous about his task. As he saw a group of young women approaching to draw water, he prayed, asking G-d to show him the right woman. If he asked a young woman for water, and she also offered to water his camels, he would know that was the girl for Isaac.[15]

While he was praying, a young woman named Rebecca came with her pitcher, and when he asked her for some water, she immediately gave him a drink. "I will also draw water for your camels," she said, doing just that.

Rebecca Waters the Camels. Painting by Alexandre Cabanel.
Photo modified: zoomed in. Public Domain:
https://commons.wikimedia.org/wiki/File:Alexandre_Cabanel_-_Rebecca_et_Eli%C3%A9zer_-_1883.jpg

---

[15] Bereshit (Genesis) 11-24.

When the camels finished drinking, he gave Rebecca a gold nose ring and two gold bracelets. It turned out that she was the granddaughter of Abraham's brother Nahor. The steward negotiated a marriage with Rebecca's brother Laban and her father, Bethuel. They called Rebecca in and asked if she was willing to travel to Canaan to marry Isaac, and she agreed. After gifting the family with treasures, the steward returned to Canaan with Rebecca.

Isaac and Rebecca had twin sons, Esau and Jacob, but Esau was born first, making him the primary heir. Jacob tricked Esau out of his birthright as a young man and stole Isaac's blessing meant for Esau. When Esau vowed to kill Jacob, Rebecca sent Jacob away to her brother Laban in Haran. On his way north to Haran, Jacob dreamed of angels ascending and descending from a ladder reaching heaven. G-d spoke to Jacob, telling him that all the families of earth would be blessed through his descendants, the same thing G-d promised Abraham.

Jacob continued to Haran and encountered his beautiful cousin Rachel at the well, where she had come to water the sheep. Jacob watered the sheep for her, kissed her, and wept, telling her he was her relative. Jacob struck a deal with his uncle Laban that he would work for him for seven years as the bride price for Rachel. After seven years, Laban tricked him and gave Jacob his less attractive daughter Leah. Laban said Jacob could also marry Rachel at the end of the week if he worked another seven years for his father-in-law.[16]

Jacob, who G-d renamed Israel, had twelve sons from his two wives and two concubines, and they became the twelve tribes of Israel. Joseph was his son from his favorite wife, Rachel, and his other sons were jealous of how Israel lavished attention on the boy. One day, his brothers sold Joseph as a slave to Egyptian traders and told their father that a wild animal had attacked and killed Joseph.

Joseph endured slavery and imprisonment in Egypt, but through his gift of dream interpretation, he was finally freed to become the pharaoh's second-in-command. His actions saved Egypt from a horrific drought. When the drought hit Canaan, his brothers came to Egypt for grain and met Joseph, who forgave them for selling him to slave traders. Joseph moved his father and brothers to Egypt, and the Israelites lived there for four centuries.

---

[16] Bereshit (Genesis) 24-29.

Key Takeaways:
- ➢ Judaism is the religion of the Jews
  - o Jews believe in one G-d
  - o The scripture is the Tanakh: Torah (law), Nevi'im (prophets), Ketuvim (writings)
  - o The Talmud interprets the law and has theological commentaries by rabbis
- ➢ Main sects of Judaism
  - o Orthodox: take the Torah at face value
  - o Reformed: believe the Torah and even G-d are myths
  - o Conservative/Masorti: interpret the Torah in line with science
- ➢ What's in the Torah?
  - o Creation and the fall
  - o The great flood
  - o The patriarchs: Abraham, Isaac, Jacob (Israel), and his twelve sons

Chapter 2: Ancient Israel

Seventy Israelites entered Egypt, and two million came out four centuries later. Life in Egypt was good at first. Joseph had interpreted the pharaoh's dream and prophesied that seven years of famine would follow seven years of plenty. During the years of bumper crops, he stored the extra grain so the Egyptians could eat during the famine. They even had enough to sell to the surrounding nations, enriching Egypt. Joseph had saved Egypt and enjoyed the high regard of the pharaoh and the Egyptians.

But a new dynasty came into power in Egypt, as told in the Shemot (Exodus), the second book of the Torah. The new pharaoh knew nothing about Joseph. But he did know that the Israelites' population had exploded, and they now outnumbered the Egyptians. What would keep them from taking over Egypt? He forced the Israelites, also known as Hebrews, into backbreaking work in construction and farming to weaken and reduce their numbers. He also commanded the genocide of all male Israelite infants.

Jochebed, a Hebrew woman from the tribe of Levi, had a baby boy and hid him for three months. Finally, she put him into a basket and floated him down the Nile River, where the pharaoh's daughter found him. The princess adopted him, naming him Moses, and hired Jochebed as his nurse. When Moses grew up, G-d called him to deliver the Israelites from Egypt. But the pharaoh refused to let the enslaved

Israelites leave Egypt.[17]

G-d sent ten plagues to Egypt to change the pharaoh's mind. Water turned into blood, then frogs, lice, and flies covered the land. Pestilence, hail, and locusts killed the livestock and grain. Boils afflicted the people, and a deep darkness covered Egypt. Goshen, where the Israelites lived, was spared. Despite the first nine dreadful plagues, the pharaoh refused to let the Hebrews leave Egypt. Then came the final and most terrible plague.

Moses warned the pharaoh that all the firstborn sons in Egypt would die. The pharaoh had ordered the death of all the Israelite male infants, and now it came back to haunt him. But the pharaoh hardened his heart. Meanwhile, G-d instructed the Hebrews to observe the first Passover. Each father must select a one-year-old, unblemished male lamb for his household. At sundown on the fourteenth day of the first month, each family was to kill the lamb and put its blood on the sides and top of their house's doorframe.

They were to roast and eat the lamb that night with unleavened bread and bitter herbs. G-d said he would pass over the houses with blood on the doorframes and spare the people within. The Passover (Seder) would be a permanent festival celebrated each year for seven days to remember G-d's deliverance. That night, the Israelites closed their doors and huddled inside. Because of the blood on the door, the angel of death passed over their homes but killed every firstborn male in Egypt, even in the pharaoh's household.

This time, the pharaoh relented. After 430 years, the entire Israelite population poured out of Egypt, with 600,000 men of military age plus women and children. Assuming the men had at least one wife and two children, more than two million people left Egypt. In addition, a multitude of Egyptians left with the Israelites. Twelve tribes (actually, thirteen) marched out, the descendants of Israel's twelve sons. The tribes were Reuben, Simeon, Judah, Issachar, Zebulun, Benjamin, Dan, Naphtali, Gad, Asher, Ephraim, and Manasseh. Ephraim and Manasseh were Joseph's sons; his descendants got a double portion. The other tribe was Levi, a separate, priestly tribe that lived among the rest of the tribes as religious leaders.

---

[17] Shemot (Exodus) 1-3, Torah, *Tanakh*.

G-d led the Israelites with a pillar of cloud by day and a pillar of fire by night. After they left Egypt, the pharaoh had a change of heart, realizing Egypt had lost its massive slave force. With his vast army, he charged out against the Israelites camped beside the Red Sea. The Israelites panicked and screamed to Moses, "Is it because there are no graves in Egypt that you have taken us to die in the desert?"

But Moses reassured them, "Don't be afraid! Stand firm and see the L-rd's salvation!"[18]

As Moses raised his staff, a strong east wind blew on the sea, splitting it in half. The great multitude crossed over with walls of water on their right and left. Meanwhile, the pillar of fire moved between the Israelite and Egyptian camps, blocking the pharaoh's army as the Israelites crossed over by night. In the morning, the pharaoh saw the Israelites had escaped and followed them into the sea. But the Egyptians' chariot wheels swerved and fell off, and then the waters crashed down, covering the pharaoh's army. Moses's sister, Miriam the prophetess, led the women with their tambourines, singing and dancing.

As they crossed the desert, the Israelites complained that they had no food, and G-d said, "Behold! I am going to rain down for you bread from heaven."[19] The following morning, when the people emerged from their tents, they found the desert covered with thin flakes. The Israelites called it manna, meaning, "What is it?" Moses explained it was bread from G-d. They could bake it into bread or boil it like porridge. Each morning, they should gather enough for their family, but on the sixth day, they should gather twice as much and prepare food for two days so that they could rest on the Sabbath.

Three months after leaving Egypt, the Israelites arrived at the Sinai desert and camped next to the high, jagged Mount Sinai. Smoke enveloped the violently quaking mountain as G-d descended in fire and called to Moses in the thunder to meet him on the summit. And there, G-d gave Moses the Ten Commandments:

1. You shall not have the gods of others in My presence.
2. You shall not make for yourself a graven image. You shall neither prostrate yourself before them nor worship them, for I, the L-rd, your G-d, am a jealous G-d.

---

[18] Shemot (Exodus) 14:11-13.
[19] Shemot (Exodus) 16:4.

3. You shall not take the name of the L-rd, your G-d, in vain.
4. Remember the Sabbath day to sanctify it.
5. Honor your father and your mother in order that your days be lengthened on the land that the L-rd, your G-d, is giving you.
6. You shall not murder.
7. You shall not commit adultery.
8. You shall not steal.
9. You shall not bear false witness against your neighbor.
10. You shall not covet your neighbor's house. You shall not covet your neighbor's wife, his manservant, his maidservant, his ox, his donkey, or whatever belongs to your neighbor.[20]

Moses and the Ten Commandments by Tissot
https://commons.wikimedia.org/wiki/File:Tissot_Moses_and_the_Ten_Commandments.jpg

    G-d also gave instructions to build the Mishkan: the tent of worship, which the Israelites carried with them as they traveled, assembling and dissembling it at each stop. In addition to the Ten Commandments, G-d gave other commandments recorded in the Torah, which fall into three broad categories. The most important laws dealt with the people's relationship with G-d, covered in the first four of the Ten Commandments.

---

[20] Shemot (Exodus) 20.

Next were laws about their relationships with each other, which included five through ten of the Ten Commandments. They also had rules relating to health and hygiene. These included the dietary laws, which forbade eating disease-carrying animals. Another law dealt with human waste disposal. They had to go to a designated place outside the camp, dig a hole, and then cover their excrement.[21]

Finally, it was time to enter Canaan and possess the land. The books of Yehoshua (Joshua) and Shoftim (Judges) in the Nevi'im section of the Tanakh tell how the twelve tribes of Israel conquered the cities one by one and divided up the land. They had to contend with the Canaanites, Hittites, and Amorites, who had lived in Canaan in Abraham's day. The Israelites subdued the Canaanites, forcing them to pay tribute but permitting them to live among them. The Philistines, who had settled along the coast while the Israelites were in Egypt, persistently raided their farmland.

The Philistines had adopted the Semitic god Dagan, the grain deity and the father of Baal (Bel), an important god in Mesopotamia and the primary god of the Canaanites. Ashtoreth, the goddess of the sea and fertility, was Baal's wife. The Torah warned the Israelites not to worship these other gods or sacrifice their children to Molek (Molech), an Ammonite god. Abraham abandoned the polytheism of his father to serve one deity only. But in Egypt, some Israelites had strayed into worshiping Egyptian gods. G-d made it clear that they should worship only לִיהוָה (YHVH) to receive his blessing and guidance. If they turned to other gods, they would suffer calamities. The Israelites vowed to follow only G-d but kept straying to Baal and Molek.

When the Israelites first returned to Canaan around 1400 BCE, they were a loose confederation of tribes with no monarch or central administration. Valiant heroes rose to fight their enemies, and their exploits are in the book of Shoftim (Judges) in the Nevi'im. Deborah was a judge who led the tribes of Naphtali and Zebulun against the Canaanites and prevailed. Gideon led three hundred men against the coalition forces of the Amalekites and Midianites with a stunning victory. G-d gave Samson supernatural strength to defeat the Philistines, but he kept getting distracted by beautiful Philistine women, which proved his undoing.

---

[21] Devarim (Deuteronomy) 23:13-15

The book of Shmuel (I & II Samuel) in the Nevi'im records the history of Israel's first two kings, Saul and David. The twelve tribes united into a monarchy around 1020 BCE, and their first king was Saul, the tallest man in Israel. While he was reigning, a boy named David was herding sheep in the fields outside Bethlehem, playing his harp and fighting off bears and lions. Saul led the Israelites in a battle against the Philistines but was stymied when they sent out their champion, a nine-foot-tall giant named Goliath. Everyone was afraid to fight him. When David visited the front lines with food for his older brothers, who were soldiers, he heard Goliath's taunts and told King Saul he would fight the giant.

"You're just a boy!" Saul protested.

David & Goliath by Schindler
https://commons.wikimedia.org/wiki/File:Osmar_Schindler_-_David_und_Goliath.jpg

But David was confident he could kill the giant. He marched out with his slingshot as Goliath laughed. But David retorted, "You come to me with sword, spear, and javelin, and I come to you with the Name of the L-rd of Hosts, the G-d of the armies of Israel which you have taunted."

David ran toward Goliath, killed the giant with the first stone from his sling, and used the giant's sword to cut Goliath's head off.[22] David later became the second king of Israel and conquered Jerusalem, making it Israel's religious and political capital. He brought the holy Ark of the Covenant to Jerusalem, which held the tablets with the Ten Commandments G-d had inscribed at Mount Sinai.

The account of the rest of the kings of Israel and Judah is recorded in Melachim (I & II Kings) in the Nevi'im. King Solomon, David's son, the wisest of men, built the First Temple (Solomon's Temple) in Jerusalem. While everyone else worshiped in the courtyard, only the priests were permitted inside the temple section called Hechal, where the Altar of Incense and Menorah stood. Only the high priest could enter through the curtain into the smaller room called Devir, or Holy of Holies, which held the Ark of the Covenant. One day a year, the high priest entered the Holy of Holies on Yom Kippur, the Day of Atonement, bringing the blood of an unblemished lamb to atone for the nation's sins.

The Kingdom of Israel unraveled immediately after Solomon's death. The Israelites sent delegates to his son, King Rehoboam, asking him to lighten the heavy tax load and enforced labor Solomon had inflicted. Rehoboam's council of elders encouraged him to lighten the load; if so, he would have the lifelong loyalty of the people. But his young friends advised him to take a tough approach. So, Rehoboam told the delegates: "My father made your yoke heavy, and I shall add to your yoke; my father flogged you with whips, and I shall flog you with scorpions."[23]

This harsh reply impelled ten Israelite tribes to split off, forming a divided kingdom. Only the tribes of Judah and Benjamin were left in the southern Kingdom of Judah under Rehoboam, with Jerusalem as its capital. The Kingdom of Israel in the north followed a polytheistic religion until its fall, but the Kingdom of Judah vacillated between the monotheistic worship of YHVH and polytheism.

---

[22] Shmuel I (I Samuel) 17, Nevi'im, *Tanakh*.
[23] Melachim I (I Kings) 12:14, Nevi'im, *Tanakh*.

Divided Kingdom: Israel in the north and Judah in the south
Oldtidens_Israel_&_Judea.svg: FinnWikiNoderivative work: Richardprins, CC BY-SA 3.0
<https://creativecommons.org/licenses/by-sa/3.0>, via Wikimedia Commons;
https://commons.wikimedia.org/wiki/File:Kingdoms_of_Israel_and_Judah_map_830.svg

The two kingdoms coexisted uneasily for the next two centuries, sometimes fighting each other and sometimes allying to fight a common enemy. In 1993, a black basalt stele (stone) was discovered in Tel Dan in northern Israel dating to the 9th century BCE. The Aramaic inscription says that Arameans warred against Israel and Judah, defeating Israel's King Joram, son of Ahab, and King Ahaziah of the "House of David."[24] The Tanakh gives an account of Joram and Ahaziah allied against the

---

[24] Nadav Na'aman, "Three Notes on the Aramaic Inscription from Tel Dan," *Israel Exploration Journal* 50, no. 1/2 (2000): 92-104. http://www.jstor.org/stable/27926919.

Aramean King Hazael. Then Jehu, from David's line, killed both Joram and Ahaziah and usurped Israel's throne, yet was defeated by King Hazael of Aram.[25] Another 9th-century BCE stele found in Dhiban, Jordan, records the victories of King Mesha of Moab over the "House of David."[26]

In the 8th century BCE, the Assyrian Tiglath-Pileser III crushed the Kingdom of Israel. He and his successor, Shalmaneser V, forced the ten tribes into exile in the Assyrian population relocation program. The Israelites resettled in the cities of Halah and Habor (in today's Syria, near Turkey's border) and in the cities of the Medes, probably north of Halah and Habor. The Assyrians relocated some of the Babylonians they had conquered to Samaria in Israel. The Assyrian strategy was that conquered people were less likely to rebel if they were removed from their homeland.

The Kingdom of Judah stumbled along until 609 BCE when Pharoah Necho II of Egypt headed north to assist the Assyrians. The Babylonians had united with the Scythians, Medes, and Persians and were annihilating Assyria. To Necho's annoyance, King Josiah of Judah refused passage through his country, so the pharaoh killed Josiah and annexed Judah as a vassal kingdom. Judah had to pay seventy-five pounds of gold and 7,500 pounds of silver in tribute. After Necho sorted out things in Judah, it was too late to help the Assyrians, whose empire dissolved.

Four years later, the Babylonian crown prince Nebuchadnezzar II destroyed the Egyptian army, making Judah a vassal state to Babylon. The Judaeans had self-rule but had to pay tribute to Babylon. Nebuchadnezzar brought a group of royal Judaean youths to Babylon and trained them in the Chaldean literature to be magi: experts in wisdom, astronomy, astrology, and dream interpretation. Once trained, they served among his advisors. Four of these young Jewish nobles were Daniel, Hananiah, Mishael, and Azariah, who received the Babylonian names Belteshazzar, Shadrach, Meshach, and Abed-nego. Nebuchadnezzar elevated these four young men to high positions.[27]

---

[25] Melachim II (II Kings) 8-10.

[26] Jean-Philippe Delorme, "בת דוד in the Mesha Stele: A Defense of André Lemaire's Reading and Its Historical Implications," *SBL and AAR New England and Eastern Canada Region Annual Meeting* (Tufts University, Massachusetts, March 22, 2019).

[27] Daniel 1, Ketuvim, *Tanakh*.

In 597 BCE, the eighteen-year-old King Jehoiachin of Judah attempted to overthrow Babylonian control. King Nebuchadnezzar marched on Judah, captured Jehoiachin, and imprisoned him for three decades in Babylon. Nebuchadnezzar pilfered the treasures in the temple and palace and installed Jehoiachin's uncle Zedekiah as the new vassal king. Leaving the humblest people of Judah to tend the land, he took 10,000 Judaean nobility, skilled military men, and craftsmen back to Babylon.

Seven years later, Zedekiah refused to pay tribute to Babylon, resulting in catastrophe. Nebuchadnezzar laid siege to Jerusalem for two years, starving the people inside. King Zedekiah tried to creep out of the city by night but was captured and blinded; the last thing he saw was his sons' execution. This time, Nebuchadnezzar pulverized Jerusalem's walls and palace and burned Solomon's Temple to the ground. The few survivors were marched to Babylon, leaving Jerusalem desolate.

"By the rivers of Babylon, we sat and wept when we remembered Zion. On willows in its midst, we hung our harps. For there, our captors asked us for a song, and our tormentors demanded mirth, 'Sing for us of the song of Zion.' How shall we sing the song of the L-rd on foreign soil? If I forget you, O Jerusalem, may my right hand forget its skill. May my tongue cling to my palate if I do not remember you, if I do not lift Jerusalem as my highest joy."[28]

Key Takeaways:
- Egypt
  - Slavery and genocide
  - G-d calls Moses
  - Plagues and Passover
- Exodus
  - Twelve tribes
  - Crossing the Red Sea
  - Manna
- The Torah Law
  - Relationship with G-d
  - Relationships with each other
  - Health and hygiene

---

[28] Tehillim (Psalms)137:1-6, Ketuvim, *Tanakh*.

- ➢ Taking the land
  - o Canaanites and Philistines and their gods
  - o Heroes who arose to fight the Israelite's enemies
- ➢ Kingdom of Israel
  - o David and Goliath
  - o Solomon builds the First Temple
- ➢ Divided kingdom: Israel and Judah
  - o Fall of Israel, Assyrian exile
  - o Temple destroyed, the Babylonian exile of Judah

Chapter 3: The Second Temple Period (540 BCE-135 CE)

Tens of thousands of exiles from the tribes of Judah, Benjamin, and Levi now lived in Babylonia.[29] Its capital, Babylon, was probably the largest city in the world, with a population exceeding 200,000. A recent exhibit of ancient tablets sheds light on life for the Jewish exiles: they paid taxes, traded in commodities, and contributed to Babylon's recovering economy.[30] Some were in high positions; for instance, Daniel was Nebuchadnezzar's chief magi and governor of Babylonia.[31]

What happened to the Israelite tribes exiled by the Assyrians in 722 BCE? These "lost tribes" disappeared from the historical record, but most Jews of the Second Temple period believed that the ten tribes would one day return. The 1st-century CE Jewish historian Josephus said an "immense multitude" lived "beyond the Euphrates" in his day.[32]

After Nebuchadnezzar's death, two coup d'états rocked Babylon. The second brought Nabonidus to the throne, who later abandoned his throne for Arabia, leaving his son Belshazzar as regent. While Babylonia crumbled under Belshazzar's incompetent and unpopular rule, Cyrus

---

[29] Ezra 2, Ketuvim, *Tanakh*.

[30] Luke Baker, "Ancient Tablets Reveal Life of Jews in Nebuchadnezzar's Babylon," *Reuters*,

[31] Daniel 2:48-49.

[32] Flavius Josephus, *The Antiquities of the Jews*, trans. William Whiston (Project Gutenberg EBook), Book XI: Chapter 5. https://www.gutenberg.org/files/2848/2848-h/2848-h.htm

the Great's Persian Empire was rapidly swallowing western Asia. When Cyrus approached Babylonia, the Babylonian troops headed north to their border wall, which extended from the Tigris to the Euphrates.

Confident that the two rivers, the troops, and the wall would hold off the Persians, Belshazzar and the rest of Babylon were celebrating the moon god festival. Belshazzar ordered the gold and silver goblets from Jerusalem's temple be brought to his banquet so everyone could drink from them. Suddenly, Belshazzar's face turned white as he saw a disembodied hand inscribing something on the wall. His mother urged him to call for Daniel, "in whom is the spirit of the gods."

Writing on the Wall by Rembrandt
https://commons.wikimedia.org/wiki/File:Belshazzar%E2%80%99s_feast,_by_Rembrandt.jpg

The elderly Daniel entered the banquet hall and informed Belshazzar, "You were weighed on the scales and found wanting. Your kingdom has been broken up and given to Media and Persia."[33]

By this time, Cyrus's army had waded across the Tigris River into Babylonia's northern frontier and marched toward Babylon at lightning speed. While Belshazzar banqueted, the Medes and Persians diverted the Euphrates, crossed over, and crashed through Babylon's Enlil gate. The Babylonians were drunk from the holiday festivities, and with little resistance, the Medes and Persians broke into the palace. They killed

---

[33] Daniel 5.

Belshazzar, and Cyrus the Great entered Babylon as its new king in 539 BCE.[34]

Cyrus permitted the populations displaced by the Assyrians and Babylonians to return to their home countries. Many Jews in high positions remained in Babylon or moved to Persia to serve Cyrus. However, 42,000 left for Jerusalem under the leadership of Judah's Prince Sheshbazzar. Cyrus returned the gold and silver utensils Nebuchadnezzar had taken from Solomon's Temple and ordered the tribes of Judah and Benjamin to rebuild it. The cost would come from the royal treasury and freewill offerings by the Jews.

The Jews resettled in their towns, and on the seventh month, everyone gathered in Jerusalem. The old temple was gone, but in the spot where the altar once stood, the priests built a new altar and reinstated the sacrifices and religious festivals. They purchased cedars from Lebanon to rebuild the temple and laid the new temple's foundation. Joyful shouts rang out, while the older generation remembered the grandeur of Solomon's Temple and wept.[35]

Two hundred years earlier, the Assyrians had exiled some defeated Babylonians to Samaria, thirty-five miles north of Jerusalem. The Babylonian-Samaritans began worshiping the Israelite G-d but continued to worship their own deities. The exiles from Sippara (Akkad) even burned their children in the fire to their gods. When the Jews returned from Babylon, the Samaritans volunteered to help them rebuild the temple. The Judeans refused because they didn't want to get sucked back into polytheism. The Samaritans got offended and started working against the Israelites, sending letters to the Persian kings with accusations against the Jews.

Fearing their adversaries and getting distracted by building their own houses, the Jews stopped building the temple. After the prophets Haggai and Zechariah charged the Jews to finish the temple, they resumed its construction. When this was reported to the new Persian king, Darius I, he ordered a search of the royal archives and found Cyrus's edict to rebuild Jerusalem's temple. Darius ordered the governor of the lands west of the Euphrates to pay for the temple's rebuilding from the tax

---

[34] Herodotus, *Capture of Babylon*, Livius. https://www.livius.org/articles/person/darius-the-great/sources/capture-of-babylon-herodotus/

[35] Ezra 1-3.

revenue and to not interfere with the reconstruction. Finally, the Second Temple was completed in the sixth year of Darius's reign (516 BCE).

Prophets Micah, Haggai, Malachi, and Zechariah by Charles M. Stuart
https://commons.wikimedia.org/wiki/File:The_Prophets_-_Micah,_Haggai,_Malachi,_Zechariah_(The_Story_of_the_Masterpieces).png

The Macedonian king Alexander the Great led a massive Greek coalition force to take on the Persian Empire in 334 BCE. He conquered one city after another, never losing a battle. The Jews in Jerusalem were terrified of Alexander because they had supported Persia when it invaded Greece in the earlier Greco-Persian Wars. According to Josephus and the Talmud, the Samaritans asked Alexander for permission to destroy Jerusalem's temple, and he gave it. So, the Jewish high priest Shimon HaTzaddik (Simon the Just) draped himself in his priestly vestments and went to meet Alexander, walking through the night and arriving at sunrise. When Alexander saw HaTzaddik approaching in the glow of dawn, he stepped down from his chariot and bowed to the high priest. Alexander said he had been having visions of HaTzaddik on the battlefield.[36,37] The Second Temple was spared and became a center of pilgrimage for Jews scattered through North Africa,

---

[36] Yoma 61 A, *Babylonian Talmud*. The William Davidson Edition. Sefaria. https://www.sefaria.org/texts/Talmud
[37] Josephus, *Antiquities of the Jews*, Book XI, Chapter 8.

the Middle East, and the Greek world.

Alexander's unexpected death in 323 BCE thrust his massive new empire into chaos. His generals divided it into separate realms, and the province of Coele-Syria, which included Judea, became part of the Seleucid Empire. The Jews had a measure of self-rule, following the laws of the Torah. Some Jerusalem Jews achieved Greek citizenship after 175 BCE, after the high priest Jason's petition.[38]

The official language for Alexander's former empire was now Koine Greek, which enabled people from Asia, North Africa, and Europe to communicate efficiently. Scholars gathered in intellectual hotspots—especially Alexandria, Egypt—to discuss science, philosophy, and religion. Egypt's Macedonian pharaoh, Ptolemy II, secluded seventy-two Jewish scholars on an island to translate the Tanakh from Hebrew into Greek.

The new Greek version of the Tanakh (Old Testament), which included the Apocrypha books, was known as the Septuagint and placed in the Library of Alexandra. Most Jews no longer spoke Hebrew, but they did know Koine Greek, so the Septuagint soon became used in the synagogues (local places for Jewish worship). Jesus read the Septuagint in Nazareth's synagogue (Luke 4:17-21).

Were the ancient Jews literate? The book of Devarim (Deuteronomy) commanded fathers to diligently teach the Torah to their children and write its verses on their houses' doorposts and gates.[39] Handwriting analysis of tablets in a remote Jewish fort south of Jerusalem indicates widespread literacy in the late 7th century BCE. On these tablets, twelve authors wrote eighteen texts dealing with mundane administrative affairs. The texts reveal that the fort's officers, the quartermaster Eliashib, and his assistant Nahum were all literate.[40] In the Second Temple period, Ezra the Scribe organized a school in Jerusalem for boys who had no father to teach them to read the Torah. And, in 64 CE, the high priest Joshua ben Gamla opened schools in every town for

---

[38] John van Maaren, *The Boundaries of Jewishness in the Southern Levant 200 BCE–132 CE* (Boston: De Gruyter, 2022), 43-108. https://doi.org/10.1515/9783110787450-002

[39] Devarim (Deuteronomy) 6:7-9, Torah, *Tanakh*.

[40] Arie Shaus, et al, "Forensic Document Examination and Algorithmic Handwriting Analysis of Judahite Biblical Period Inscriptions Reveal Significant Literacy Level," *PLOS One* (September 9, 2020). https://doi.org/10.1371/journal.pone.0237962

boys.[41]

In 246 BCE, Ptolemy III of Egypt wrested Coele-Syria, including Judea, from the Seleucid Empire. In 200 BCE, Antiochus III (the Great) of the Seleucid Empire schemed with Philip V of Macedonia to overthrow Egypt, which was in crisis. The new pharaoh was only six years old, and his family members were clashing over who should be the regent. Antiochus the Great successfully took Coele-Syria back from Egypt, and the Jews threw open the gates of Jerusalem to welcome him. Little did they know the horrors to come.

Rome was a rising power in the region when Antiochus IV Epiphanes usurped the throne from his nephew at Antiochus the Great's death. Antiochus IV wanted to impose a totalitarian Hellenistic (Greek) culture and religion. He sold the high priest position to Menelaus, who was willing to syncretize Judaism with Greek ways. Antiochus dipped into the temple treasury to fund his war against Egypt. Meanwhile, Egypt tried to take back Coele-Syria, but Antiochus Epiphanes successfully quelled its initial effort. He marched on Egypt again in 168 BCE.

But the Roman envoy Popillius blocked his way, holding orders from the Roman Senate. "Leave Egypt immediately, or you will be at war with Rome." The elderly proconsul drew a circle in the sand around Antiochus. "Stay in that circle until you give me an answer for the Senate."

Sputtering in rage, the humiliated Antiochus Epiphanes left Egypt. As he passed through Judea, he took out his pent-up fury on Jerusalem after discovering the Jews had replaced Menelaus with their previous high priest. He slaughtered forty thousand men, women, and children in three days and reinstated Menelaus. When a second revolt broke out, Antiochus outlawed Judaism. He installed a statue of Zeus in the temple and sacrificed a pig, an unclean animal to the Jews.

This outrage triggered the Maccabean Revolt in 167 BCE, led by a priest named Mattathias and his military men called the Maccabees (meaning hammer). They launched guerilla warfare against the Greeks and Hellenized Jews, destroying idols around Judea. Although outnumbered by at least five to one, they defeated the Seleucid army, retook Jerusalem, and purified the temple, rededicating it to G-d. In December 164 BCE, they celebrated the first Festival of Lights

---

[41] Bava Batra 21a, *Babylonian Talmud*.

(Chanukah or Hannukah).

Judea was now essentially independent of the crumbling Seleucid Empire. The Jewish leaders of the new Hasmonaean dynasty served dual roles of high priest and king. The Hasmonaean dynasty increased its territory five-fold, taking back Galilee and other provinces of the former Kingdom of Israel. But it all fell apart in 67 BCE when Aristobulus II stole the throne and priesthood from his brother, King Hyrcanus. Hyrcanus's advisor, Antipater the Idumean, recommended allying with Aretas III of Arabia and retaking the throne.

Meanwhile, Rome's consul Pompey was in western Asia, conquering the territories of the collapsed Seleucid Empire. He arrived in Judea just as the armies of Hyrcanus and the Arabians were surrounding Jerusalem. Pompey put the Arabians to flight, then broke into the temple and captured Aristobulus. He reinstalled Hyrcanus as high priest but not as king. Shortly after, Julius Caesar appointed Antipater the Idumean as Judea's Roman procurator (governor), although he wasn't ethnically Jewish.

Model of the Second Temple
M.t.lifshits, CC BY-SA 3.0 <https://creativecommons.org/licenses/by-sa/3.0>, via Wikimedia Commons; https://commons.wikimedia.org/wiki/File:Model_of_Jerusalem_in_the_Late_Second_Temple_Period.JPG

In 37 BCE, the Roman Senate made Antipater's son, Herod the Great, the king of Judaea, now Rome's vassal kingdom. The Hasmoneans had enlarged the temple, and Herod refurbished and enlarged it more with Greek-style Corinthian columns. Herod executed the surviving members of the Hasmonean dynasty, including his wife Mariamme and his two sons by her. Herod the Great is the king that the

New Testament says killed all the baby boys in Bethlehem in an attempt to kill the infant Jesus (Matthew 2).

The Jewish historian Josephus wrote about Jesus, although some scholars suspect his text may have been edited later:

"Now there was about this time Jesus, a wise man if it be lawful to call him a man; for he was a doer of wonderful works, a teacher of such men as receive the truth with pleasure. He drew over to him both many of the Jews and many of the Gentiles. He was [the] Christ. And when Pilate, at the suggestion of the principal men amongst us, had condemned him to the cross, those that loved him at the first did not forsake him; for he appeared to them alive again the third day; as the divine prophets had foretold these and ten thousand other wonderful things concerning him. And the tribe of Christians, so named from him, are not extinct at this day."[42]

The Second Temple, built by the returned exiles from Babylon, was Judea's center of worship for four centuries. Through this period, the Jews experienced internal conflict between various factions. The Pharisees carefully followed religious rituals, separating themselves from the Hellenistic Jews and others who failed to follow the Torah strictly. The Sadducees allied with the Romans, often buying high positions like high priest. They did not believe in heaven or hell or life after death. The Zealots were fanatical nationalists who wanted to overthrow Roman rule.

In 66 CE, the Jews rioted against their cruel Roman governor Florus, who retaliated by killing 3,600 Jews in Jerusalem, sparking a revolt throughout Judaea led by the Zealots. The Roman emperor sent General Vespasian to quell the uprising, and he brutally crushed the resistance fighters in Judaea's northern regions. Meanwhile, Jerusalem erupted into civil war between the Zealots and other factions. Amid this chaos, Emperor Nero died, and the Senate appointed Vespasian as Rome's new emperor. Vespasian returned to Rome in 69 CE, leaving his son Titus to finish Judaea's subjugation. Titus marched on Jerusalem with eighty thousand men just as thousands of Jews had traveled to the city for Passover.

The Zealots had divided into two warring groups: the extreme and the moderate. The extreme Zealots attacked the moderate Zealots and other

---

[42] Josephus, *Antiquities of the Jews*, Book XVIII, Chapter 3.

worshipers celebrating Passover in the temple courtyard, killing most of the moderates. Outside Jerusalem's walls, Titus launched his attack. Outnumbered four to one, the Jewish factions finally stopped killing each other to face their common enemy.

With their battering rams and catapults, the Romans broke down Jerusalem's northern wall after two weeks. As they fought their way toward the center of the city and the temple mount, the Jews dug a tunnel under their siege equipment and burned their catapults and battering rams. Titus built a wall around the unconquered section of the city to starve the Jews. Josephus, who had been captured by the Romans and was serving as a negotiator, wrote:

"Then did the famine widen its progress and devoured the people by whole houses and families; the upper rooms were full of women and children that were dying by famine, and the lanes of the city were full of the dead bodies of the aged; the children also and the young men wandered about the market-places like shadows, all swelled with the famine, and fell down dead, wheresoever their misery seized them."[43]

Titus continued pressing toward the temple, where most of the survivors huddled. His men set it on fire, and for two days, it burned, with many Jews still inside. All that remained of the temple was the retaining wall on the western temple mount. The surviving Jews were enslaved or sent to fight wild animals to entertain the people of Rome.

The diaspora, or dispersion of the Jews, to other regions outside Judaea had begun with the Assyrian and Babylonian exiles. Although thousands of Jews returned from Babylon when freed by Cyrus the Great, many remained in Assyria, Babylon, and Persia. During the Hellenistic age, thousands of Jewish intellectuals migrated to Egypt, where Alexandria was the scientific and philosophical hub. After the fall of Jerusalem in 70 CE, Jews left for places like Egypt, Babylon, or Persia, which already had large Jewish populations. Because they spoke Koine Greek, other Jews migrated throughout the Greek world surrounding the eastern Mediterranean.

Jews had arrived in Rome by the 2nd century BCE. By the end of the 1st century CE, at least two million lived in the Roman Empire as the diaspora spread through southern Europe and northern Africa. As

---

[43] Flavius Josephus, *The Wars of the Jews*, trans. William Whiston (Project Gutenberg EBook), Book V, Chapter 12. https://www.gutenberg.org/files/2850/2850-h/2850-h.htm

Josephus wrote: "This people has already made its way into every city, and it is not easy to find any place in the habitable world which has not received the nation and in which it has not made its power felt."[44]

Key Takeaways:
- Babylonian and Persian rule
  - Tribes of Judah and Benjamin in Babylon
  - Cyrus the Great overthrows Babylon
- Return to Jerusalem and the Second Temple
  - Cyrus's order to rebuild the temple
  - The Second Temple completed in 516 BCE
- Alexander the Great and the Hellenistic period
  - Tanakh translated into Koine Greek
  - Schools established for boys to learn the Torah
- Maccabean Revolt, Jewish autonomy, Hasmonean dynasty
  - Desecration of the temple
  - Expansion to include most of former Israel
- Roman rule
  - Pompey's conquest
  - Herod's Temple
  - Jesus
  - Revolt and destruction of Jerusalem and temple
- Diaspora movements

---

[44] Josephus, *Antiquities of the Jews*. Book XIV, Chapter 7.

Chapter 4: Byzantine Judaism (324-640CE)

Writing down the Mishna, the Oral Law, was forbidden at one time. What is the Oral Law? It is the unwritten law the rabbis believe Moses received from G-d when he received the written Torah. The Mishna helps to interpret the Torah. Why couldn't it be written down? The rabbis explained that a medical student couldn't learn his profession simply by reading textbooks. He must observe a master physician and then have that master guide him through his first surgeries. How could one understand the Mishna simply by reading and not interacting with a master teacher? How would one know how to apply its teachings to the rapidly changing world?

But the rapidly changing world was the problem with learning the Mishna from a master teacher. The Jews were scattered to the four winds, and not everyone had access to a master teacher.

Rabbi Judah HaNasi of Galilee was a close friend of the Roman emperor but knew that the empire's benign treatment of the Jews could change in the blink of an eye. How soon before a new emperor came to power and the Jews were scattered again? So, Rabbi Judah gathered the leading Torah scholars. They spent years analyzing the Oral Law and writing it down with commentaries explaining the teachings. They attempted to resolve disputes among the leading sages on how to interpret the Oral Law. Completed around 200 CE, the Mishna contains instructions on prayer, religious rituals, the Sabbath, special holy days, and how to mourn. It gives regulations on agriculture, marriage and divorce, financial affairs, and court matters.

Around 350 CE, rabbinic scholars completed the Jerusalem Gemara, a collection of discussions by rabbis. They were still reviewing and revising it, but the Romans shut down any scholarly work in Jerusalem. The Gemara, together with the Mishna, formed the Jerusalem Talmud. Many rabbis escaped to Babylon, where Jewish scholars were also developing a written Talmud. The rabbis continued reviewing and expanding the Talmud for decades. At some point in the 400s, they completed the Babylonian Talmud, which is usually considered more authoritative.

The Talmud Readers by Adolf Behrman, who was killed by the Nazis in 1943 in Poland's Białystok Ghetto
https://commons.wikimedia.org/wiki/File:Adolf_Behrman_-_Talmudysci.jpg

Judaism in the Roman Empire

The necessity of writing down the Mishna underscored the turbulent relationship the Jews had with the Roman Empire. Sometimes they enjoyed favor from the emperor, and sometimes they received cruelty and oppression. It all depended on who the emperor was and how much the Jews were resisting Roman rule. For instance, when Emperor Hadrian rebuilt Jerusalem in 132 CE, he built a temple to Jupiter where the First and Second Temples once stood, sparking a revolt led by

Simon bar Kokhba. Hadrian's forces killed 580,000 Jews, enslaved or exiled thousands more, and demolished 1,000 towns. Hadrian outlawed Judaism, forbade circumcision, and burned the Torah. He merged the province of Judaea with Galilee and called it Syria Palaestina.

However, Hadrian's successor, Antoninus Pius, repealed many of Hadrian's harsh policies against the Jews. He permitted them to follow Judaism but not convert others to their religion. Jews were still banned from Jerusalem. In 193 CE, Severus became Rome's military dictator. A North African of Semitic-Phoenician descent, he initiated a new dynasty. During Severus's reign, Jews could hold public office but were still forbidden to convert others to Judaism. Severus's son Caracalla even permitted free Jews to obtain full Roman citizenship. Another Severan emperor, Alexander, allowed the Jews to visit Jerusalem.

Nevertheless, during the Severan dynasty (191-235 CE), the Jews and Christians in the empire suffered sporadic persecution in some of the provinces, albeit not directly from the emperors. The reason was that being a loyal subject of the Roman Empire meant accepting the Roman gods. Since most people within the empire were already polytheistic before being conquered, they simply shrugged and added the Roman gods to their pantheon. Sometimes they renamed their own gods with the names of the chief Roman gods. Yet the Jews and Christians refused to offer sacrifices to any other god or observe pagan religious festivals, which made them seem disloyal to the government.

In 313 CE, Constantine and his co-emperor Licinius passed the Edict of Milan, which protected all religions (including Christianity and Judaism) from persecution. In 315 CE, Constantine passed a law forbidding Jews from stoning a fellow Jew who converted to Christianity. The punishment for disobeying was death in the flames. Constantine also forbade non-Jews from attending synagogue or converting to Judaism.

Influenced by his Christian mother, Constantine studied the Christian faith, although he did not receive baptism until his deathbed. His mother, Helena, drew attention to Jerusalem and Palestine and the location of specific events in the life of Jesus. Helena and Constantine built several cathedrals in Jerusalem as Palestine morphed from an obscure Roman province into a center of pilgrimage. Monasteries for ascetic hermits soon dotted the Judaean landscape.

Judaism in the Byzantine era

In 324 CE, Constantine I became the sole emperor of the Roman Empire. Rome became a backwater and was no longer the capital of the empire. Constantine built his new capital of Constantinople, where Europe meets Asia on the Bosphorus Strait. The Western Roman Empire crumbled over the next two centuries and eventually collapsed, while the Eastern Roman Empire, known today as the Byzantine Empire, flourished.

In 325 CE, Constantine I convened the First Ecumenical Council at Nicaea, which hashed out some Christian doctrinal issues and changed the date of Easter, previously celebrated at Passover. Constantine didn't like a Christian festival connected with a Jewish one.

In 339 CE, Constantine's son Constantius II passed a law dissolving marriages between Jewish men and non-Jewish women employed in the imperial weaving factory. If Jewish men married non-Jewish women in the future, they would be executed. The law forbade Jews from owning non-Jewish slaves, and circumcising an enslaved male brought the death penalty. Theodosius I (347-395 CE) promoted Christian missionary activity among the Jews and forbade Jewish parents from disinheriting their children who converted to Christianity. However, when Christians burned down a synagogue in Callinicum, Syria, in 388 CE, Theodosius ordered the perpetrators punished and forced them to return all stolen property. In 439 CE, Theodosius II forbade building new synagogues, although old synagogues could be repaired and refurbished. If a Jew influenced a Christian to convert to Judaism, he would lose his property and life.[45]

Despite oppression, Judaism grew during the Byzantine period.

---

[45] Jacob Marcus, *The Jew in the Medieval World: A Sourcebook, 315-1791* (New York: Jewish Publication Society, 1938), 3-7.

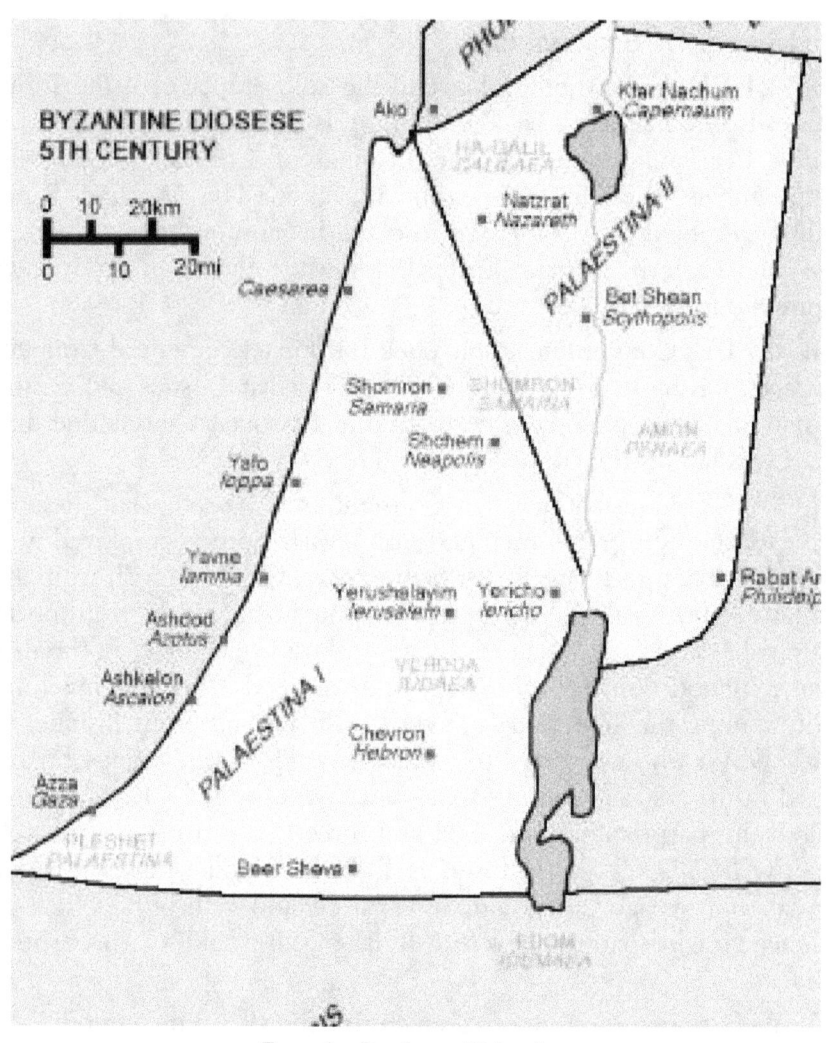

Byzantine Province of Palaestina
Photo modified: zoomed in. Credit: Haldrik at https://en.wikipedia.org/;
https://commons.wikimedia.org/wiki/File:Israel_Byzantine_5c.jpg

Judaism's leadership became decentralized in the Byzantine era, focusing on local governance. Jewish communities throughout the empire had their own leadership: scholars chosen from influential and wealthy families. Jewish merchants plied their trade by land and sea, and cloth dyeing became a noted Jewish occupation. The province roughly covering the former kingdoms of Israel and Judah was split in two. Jerusalem was in Palaestina I to the south, and Galilee in the northern Palaestina II.

Palaestina continued as the Jewish cultural center, with significant creative endeavors in Hebrew liturgical poetry. The Jewish poets or *payṭanim*, such as Yose ben Yose, Yannai, and Eleazar ha-Kalir, echoed the ancient psalmists with fervent devotion and a passionate longing for the Messiah. Romanos, a monk who had converted from Judaism to Christianity, employed the payṭanim style in the Byzantine worship liturgy.

Judaism in North Africa

The Jewish people always had a strong connection to Africa, especially Egypt and Ethiopia (Cush). The Torah mentions Abraham and Isaac migrating to Egypt during famines, and Jacob and his sons moved there when Joseph was Egypt's second-in-command. The Jewish prophets, such as Zephaniah, frequently spoke of Ethiopia: "From the other side of the rivers of Cush, My supplicants, the community of My scattered ones, shall bring Me an offering."[46]

The Beta Israel Jewish artisans and agriculturalists of northern Ethiopia's mountains along the Gerzeman River formed the mysterious Kingdom of Semien. How and when they came to Ethiopia is unclear. It must have been before 70 CE, as they still practiced animal sacrifice and knew nothing about the Mishna or Talmud. Isolated from other Jews until the 19th century, they developed a distinct culture. Their ascetic high priests, the *meloksewoch*, are reminiscent of the Essenes sect of the 1st century CE who wrote the Dead Sea Scrolls.

The Beta Israel Jews often conflicted with the mostly Christian Ethiopians in the Byzantine era, although they maintained political autonomy. They eventually lost their farmland when the Ethiopian monarchy only permitted Christians to be landowners. But they were skilled in craftsmanship and masonry and helped build Ethiopia's new capital of Gondor in 1632.[47]

The Maghrebi Jews also lived in North Africa from at least the 1st century CE; however, they maintained contact with Jerusalem and the rest of the Jewish world. Found in Morocco, Algeria, Tunisia, and Libya, some of these Jews were descendants of the 30,000 deported by Titus

---

[46] Tzefaniah (Zephaniah) 3:10, Nevi'im, *Tanakh*.

[47] Sara Toth Stub, "Letter from Ethiopia: Exploring a Forgotten Jewish Land," *Archaeology*. January/February 2023. https://www.archaeology.org/issues/498-2301/letter-from/11057-ethiopia-beta-israel

after the 70 CE fall of Jerusalem. However, a Jewish settlement already existed in Cyrene (in Libya), as the New Testament mentions that the Roman soldiers forced Simon of Cyrene to carry Jesus's cross. The original El Ghriba Synagogue on the island of Djerba in Tunisia was supposedly built with a door and stone from the destroyed temple in Jerusalem. One version of the legend says they were from the Second Temple, but another version insists these relics came from Solomon's Temple, destroyed by Nebuchadnezzar in 586 BCE.

Judaism in the Middle East

As mentioned earlier, after Cyrus the Great conquered Babylon, he granted citizenship to the Jews and permission to return to Jerusalem. While tens of thousands returned to their homeland, thousands chose to stay in Babylon. An ancient synagogue in Nehardea on the Euphrates was said to have been built by the exiled King Jehoiachin. After the 70 CE fall of Jerusalem, many Jews left for Babylonia (in today's Iraq), which became the academic center of Judaism. Rabbinical schools flourished, and the kallah (general assembly) met twice a year for scholars to debate theological issues.

The Christianization of the Byzantine Empire led to another exodus of Jews to Babylonia, which was now part of the Persian Sasanian Empire. In 512 CE, Mar Zutra II, the exilarch (leader) of the Jewish community, challenged the Sasanians, who had killed his father and other family members. His four hundred Jewish warriors defeated the Persians of the area, and Mar Zutra established an independent Jewish state in Mahoza on the banks of the Tigris. After seven years, the Persian king Kavadh I defeated Mar Zutra and crucified him.

From 484 to 573 CE, the Samaritans north of Jerusalem launched a series of insurrections against Byzantine rule in Palaestina I (today's southern Israel). Most Jews had left Palaestina I after the Bar Kokhba revolt, except for Caesarea on the northern coast. The Jews were still the majority in Palaestina II in Galilee and Golan, while the Samaritans and Byzantine Christians dominated Palaestina I. The Samaritans had their temple on Mount Gerizim and practiced a hybrid form of Judaism.

The Byzantine emperor Zeno persecuted the Samaritans, trying to force them to convert to Christianity. When they refused, he turned one of their synagogues into a church, and on Mount Gerizim, he built a tomb for his son with a cross on it. In 484 CE, the Samaritans retaliated by storming the cathedral at Neapolis and killing the Christians worshiping inside. Zeno marched on Samaria and quelled the rebellion. He forbade the Samaritans from setting foot on Mount Gerizim and built a church there. Continuing to revolt for almost a century, the Samaritans lost tens of thousands in their struggle against the Byzantine Empire.

In 556 CE, the Jews got involved. With the Samaritans, they attacked the Christians of Caesarea, raiding the churches and killing the governor. The rebellion spread to Bethlehem, where the Samaritan-Jewish coalition burned down the Church of the Nativity. In 572 CE, the Jews joined the Samaritans again in another insurrection at Mount Carmel. After this, the Byzantines outlawed the Samaritan religion, and the Samaritan population became nearly extinct.

Although they must have likewise suffered the wrath of the Byzantine Empire following the Samaritan revolts, a sizeable Jewish population continued in Caesarea. In 615 CE, Shahrbaraz, shah of the Sassanian Empire, conquered Caesarea, which was now the capital of Palaestina I. The Jews from Palaestina I and II allied with the Persian forces against the Byzantines and took Jerusalem but failed to take Tyre. In 622 CE, the Byzantine emperor Heraclius counterattacked and regained Jerusalem.

Meanwhile, in Arabia, Muhammad was having revelations in a cave and starting a new religion. He died in 632 CE, but his followers continued his quest to spread Islam. In 638 CE, Jerusalem surrendered to the Muslims led by Caliph Umar with a treaty that protected the lives and property of the city's citizens. Heraclius had banned the Jews from entering Jerusalem, but Umar allowed them to return with certain restrictions. For instance, neither Jews nor Christians could hold government offices; Jews could not build new synagogues, and Christians could not erect new churches. But now, the Jews could pray at the Temple Mount and Western Wall (Wailing Wall) in Jerusalem.

Key Takeaways:
- Codification of Mishna and Jerusalem and Babylonian Talmud completed
- The turbulent life of Jews in the Roman Empire
    - Mixed relationship depending on who the emperor was
    - Impact of Constantine and the legalization of Christianity

- The growth of Judaism during the Byzantine period (320-640CE).
  - Initial decline; conversion attempts by Christians
  - Judaism in North Africa
- Jews in the Middle East
  - Babylonia the scholarly center of Judaism
  - Samaritan insurrections and Jewish involvement
  - 615 CE Sassanian invasion
  - 636 CE beginning of Arab rule

Chapter 5: Medieval Judaism I: Islam and the Spanish Golden Age

After the devastating Jewish-Roman wars, a Jewish tribe called the Banu Qurayza moved into western Arabia in the region later called Medina. They introduced the cultivation of date palms, grains, and vineyards, lifting the Jews to a high social standing among the Bedouin Arabs, who were primarily sheep and camel herdsmen. These Jews followed the Torah but intermarried with Arabs and allied with the local Arab tribes in warfare against other tribes. The Arabs called the Banu Qurayza Jews the "kahinan," or priestly tribe. When the Sasanians gained power in Arabia, the Banu Qurayza Jews served as tax collectors for the Persians.

Several other Jewish tribes, including the Banu Qaynuqa and Banu Nadir, also moved into Medina. The Arab tribes around Medina were constantly at war with each other, and the Jewish tribes joined the fray. The prophet Muhammed and his followers migrated to Medina in 622 CE and mediated peace among the tribes with the Constitution of Medina. It assured freedom of religious belief for all who followed the law. The Jews would have equality and not be oppressed or harassed.

Five years later, Muhammed's tribe, the Quraysh from Mecca, who had not accepted Islam, allied with the Banu Nadir Jewish tribe and attacked Medina. In the Battle of the Trench, the Banu Qurayza Jews did not participate in the fighting but gave tools to Muhammed's men to dig a defensive trench. They did negotiate with the Jews fighting with the Meccans, who convinced the Medina Jews that Muhammed would lose the war. However, negotiations between the two Jewish tribes broke down, and the Medina Jews did nothing to support the attacking tribes.

Nevertheless, once the Meccans abandoned the war, Muhammed attacked the Banu Qurayza Jews, offended that they had negotiated with the attackers. About two thousand Jewish men, women, and children surrendered to him. They were invited to convert to Islam and refused. The Muslims beheaded all the Jewish men, enslaved all the women and children, and confiscated their property.

Seizure of the Banu Qurayza by Muhammad Rafi' Bāzil
https://commons.wikimedia.org/wiki/File:Ban%C5%AB_Qurayza.png

After Muhammed died and Caliph Umar came to power, he evicted all Jews from Arabia and confiscated their lands. These Jews migrated to Syria and Babylonia (Iraq). Yet when Umar invaded and conquered Palaestina, the Muslim treatment of Jews was initially benign, especially since the Jews assisted his conquest of Caesarea. The Jews established a rabbinic academy in Galilee at Tiberius. Galilee had attained spiritual supremacy after the 70 CE fall of Jerusalem, and the Sanhedrin (Assembly of Elders) had relocated to Usher in Galilee. The Muslim conquests left Anatolia (western Turkey) as the Byzantine Empire's only Asian territory.

By 686 CE, the Umayyad dynasty ruled North Africa and Syria, which now included Palestine. The Shi'ite Muslims had split off and ruled what is now Iraq and northern Iran. The Kharijites were another splinter group that controlled large areas of Persia (southern Iran) and Arabia. Since only Muslims could serve in the military, all three Muslim groups forced able-bodied non-Muslim males of military age to pay the *jizya* tax. Under Umar's rule, the amount of the tax depended on whether one was wealthy, middle-class, or poor.

Another tax imposed by the Muslims was the *kharaj* tax on the non-Muslim landowners' harvest. Muslim landowners had to pay a 10 percent tithe on their land, which was far less than the *kharaj* tax. By 750 CE, non-Muslims were paying as much as one-third of their harvest in taxes. The crushing *kharaj* taxes forced the land-owning Jews in Babylonia and elsewhere to migrate from rural farms into the cities. This mass migration resulted in most Jews becoming urban dwellers for the next millennia. These urbanized Jews grew wealthy from manufacturing and trade and became increasingly engaged in global affairs and Western philosophy.

Meanwhile, the Muslims in Jerusalem decided on the Temple Mount as their place of prayer. A few Jews could live in Jerusalem once again, but the majority population was still Christian. The Umayyad Caliph Abd al-Malik expanded Jerusalem and rebuilt its walls and roads. On the site where the First and Second Temples once stood, Caliph el-Malik built the Dome of the Rock in 693 CE and the al-Aqsa Mosque in 705 CE. Under Umar II (717-720 CE), Jews were forced to identify themselves by wearing yellow stars, and Christians had to wear blue badges.

In Eastern Europe, a nomadic people known as the Khazars roamed the steppes of today's Russia and Ukraine; they settled along the Danube in the mid-600s as far south as the Black Sea. Around 740 CE, King Bulan and the Khazar nobility converted to Judaism, followed by many of the Khazar population. King Bulan's descendants built synagogues and imported Jewish scholars to teach the Tanakh and Talmud. The Jewish teachers instructed the people to read Hebrew and celebrate Jewish festivals. This Jewish kingdom persisted for five centuries until it fell to Genghis Khan and the Mongols.

Tchufute Kalei, Fortress of the Jews, in the Crimea
Leah Lipszyc, CC BY-SA 3.0 <https://creativecommons.org/licenses/by-sa/3.0>, via Wikimedia Commons, https://commons.wikimedia.org/wiki/File:Tchufute_Kalei_tower_near_back_entrance.JPG

Jews had lived in Western Europe since the Roman era. For instance, the 1st-century apostle Paul mentioned visiting Spain (Romans 15:24). The Jews in France and other Western European states monopolized trade in silk, incense, wine, and spices, but some also owned land and were farmers. Some of the region's legislation was anti-Semitic, such as the third Council of Orleans (538 CE), which restricted Jews from appearing in public from Maundy Thursday to Easter Sunday.

In Western Europe, Charlemagne rose to power as king of the Franks. Eventually, in 800 CE, he united and ruled the Western Roman Empire, which had collapsed three centuries earlier. Charlemagne actively protected the Jews of Western Europe and encouraged the development of Jewish culture. He appointed a Jew as his ambassador to Baghdad. His son Louis the Pius continued his father's benevolent policies and granted privileges to Jewish merchants. At this point, Jews served as the intermediaries between the Christian West and the Islamic East.[48]

The Abbasid Caliphate overthrew the Umayyad dynasty in 750 CE and ruled the eastern Muslim world until conquered by the Mongols in 1258. In 762 CE, the Abbasids established their new capital at Baghdad, about fifty miles north of Babylon. They adopted the Sassanian (Persian) governmental system and promoted the arts and sciences in this "golden age" of Islamic culture.

Most Abbasid caliphs tolerated the Jews, but a few persecuted them with oppressive taxes and strict rules for their clothing and trade. For instance, Caliph al-Mutawakkil (847-861 CE) forced the Jews to wear a yellow hood or patch on their chest or back. Nevertheless, the Jews distinguished themselves under the Abbasid Caliphate as administrators, merchants, physicians, and writers.

Since the Hellenistic age, some Jews had questioned the validity of the oral law (Mishna). Around 767 CE, a Persian Jew named Anan Ben David organized the Karaite sect, which recognizes the Tanakh (Old Testament) as the highest authority for theology and law. The Karaites believe G-d gave Moses only the written Torah, not the oral Mishna. Thus, they do not consider the Talmud to be authoritative. They might consult the Talmud, but ultimately, each person was responsible for deciding how to interpret the Torah.

At this time, tension mounted between Saadia Gaon (882-942 CE), a leading Rabbinic Jewish sage in Babylonia during the Abbasid Caliphate, and Aaron ben Meir, the leading Jewish scholar in Palestine, over changing the dates of Passover and Rosh Hashanah. Saadia won the battle of the calendars, keeping the traditional dates for the festivals and highlighting Babylonian authority in the Jewish world.

Saadia translated the Tanakh (Old Testament) into Arabic, a version still used today. He also wrote a Hebrew grammar book and a dictionary to assist Jews in reading the Torah in Hebrew. Saadia authored his *Book of Beliefs and Opinions* in classic Arabic, defending Judaism and drawing Jews back to the Torah. Yet, he pointed out that the teachings of Aristotle and Plato could rationally fit in with traditional Jewish theology

---

[48] Michael G. Minsky, *Agobard and His Relations with the Jews* (Amherst: University of Massachusetts, 1971), 1-18.

and philosophy.

In 969 CE, the Fatimid Caliphate rose to power in North Africa, Syria, and Palestine (roughly today's Israel). The Fatimid were Shi'ite Muslims, who were more tolerant toward non-Muslims and even appointed Jews and Christians to administrative positions. The Jews in Asia and North Africa now had more religious freedom and positions such as court physician and clerk for the military.

Jews were active in the Fatimid economy and interacted freely with Muslims and Christians. The Jews continued their lucrative roles in textile manufacturing and trade, even supplying the court. They prospered in this era, which lasted until 1171, while continuing to pay the *jizya* tax levied against all non-Muslims. Although they adopted Muslim dress and the Arabic language, the Jews maintained their culture and religious practices. They usually settled legal affairs among themselves following Torah law, rarely taking matters to Muslim courts.

In the Fatimid Caliphate, the Jews elected one of their own as "Head of the Jews," which the caliphate approved and recognized with a letter of appointment. Muhammed had promised this for Jews and Christians, but it had not always happened under other caliphates. The power vested in the Head of the Jews included overseeing legal affairs within the Jewish community and appointing officers under him. He managed religious endowments, supervised tax collection among the Jews, and ensured that the Jewish community observed regulations for non-Muslims. The Jews chose one of their more affluent men, and this leader presided over Jews and Samaritans.[49]

Meanwhile, as the Abbasid dynasty fractured in the 10th century, many Middle Eastern Jews migrated to regions around the Mediterranean. The Umayyad Caliphate had conquered Andalusia (Spain) in 711 CE, and Muslim rule prevailed until the mid-13th century. These Muslim leaders were tolerant of Jews and Christians, opening doors for unprecedented cultural achievement in the Middle Ages. The Jews enjoyed a golden age of splendor in economic, spiritual, and cultural life from 950 to 1150 CE as Spain became the world's largest Jewish community.

---

[49] Elinoar Bareket, "The Head of the Jews (Ra'is al-Yahud) in Fatimid Egypt: A Re-Evaluation," *Bulletin of the School of Oriental and African Studies*, University of London 67, no. 2 (2004): 185-6. http://www.jstor.org/stable/4145978.

Spain's Muslim leadership appointed Jews to administrative posts and encouraged their trade endeavors. Muslim and Jewish scholars surged ahead in astronomy, mathematics, medicine, philosophy, and poetry while the rest of Europe descended into the Dark Ages. Cosmopolitan cities sprang up, with aqueducts, sewers, paved roads, splendid palaces, and breathtaking gardens. The libraries of Cordova, Granada, and Toledo drew science and math scholars.

Spanish Judaism led the Sephardic Jews of North Africa, Palestine, and the Middle East, while the Ashkenazi Jews centered in France, Germany, and Italy. These two groups differed in their prayer service, theology, and pursuit of secular knowledge. The Ashkenazim approached the Talmud analytically; the Sephardim were influenced by Arabic and Western philosophy, believing it helped to understand the Torah. The Sephardim immersed themselves in the non-Jewish world, while the Ashkenazim avoided secular studies in philosophy, science, and math and gave full attention to the Torah.

In 1027, the poet Samuel ha-Nagid became the prime minister of Granada in southern Spain and led the way for Spanish Jews in literary and political fields. Solomon Ibn Gabirol (1021-1058) was a Jewish poet and philosopher in Spain who penned the *Mekor Chayim* (*Origin of Life*) about the intersection of the earthly and spiritual world. He warned that since G-d is the true source of life, seeking satisfaction in worldly things is idolatry.

Woodcut of Rabbi Solomon ben Isaac (Rashi) by Guillaume de Paris
https://commons.wikimedia.org/wiki/File:Rashi.JPG

Rabbi Solomon ben Isaac (1040-1105), known as Rashi, was a renowned French scholar whose commentaries on the Tanakh and Talmud are still studied today by Jewish children and adults. He meticulously analyzed the meaning of the Hebrew text, paying particular attention to word studies and their literal meaning. Biblical scholars appreciated how he explained complex texts with simplicity and clarity, and his commentary is included in today's editions of the Talmud.

The golden age of the Jews in Spain ended in 1147 when the Almohad Berber Muslims of Morocco attacked the Iberian Peninsula. The Jews had mostly flourished under earlier Muslim leadership in Spain, but the radical Almohads were fanatical about imposing Islam. The Jews and Christians had three choices: convert to Islam, leave the country, or be executed. Most Jews fled to North Africa or to the north of Spain, which was under Christian control.

Meanwhile, affairs in Jerusalem were setting the scene for the Crusades. In 1071, the Fatimid Muslim governor of al-Sham (Syria-Palestine) asked the Turkmens for help fending off Arab Bedouin tribes invading the region. The Turkish Seljuks came down to fight as mercenaries, but then the Fatimids couldn't pay them due to a civil war in their Egyptian heartland. So, the Seljuks switched sides. They fought with the Bedouins, captured Jerusalem, and made it part of the Seljuk Empire. The Sunni Muslim Turks governed Jerusalem until 1098 when the Fatimid warriors retook the city.

Key Takeaways:
- ➢ Byzantine Empire loses control to Caliph Umar
  - o Migration of Babylonian Jews to the cities due to the *kharaj* land tax
  - o Dome of the Rock (693 CE) and the al-Aqsa Mosque (705 CE) built on Temple Mount
  - o Jews in the Abbasid Caliphate
    - o Anan Ben David and the Karaite sect
    - o Saadia Gaon and Babylonian leadership in the Jewish world
- ➢ Jewish life in the Fatimid Caliphate
  - o More religious freedom and opportunities for economic prosperity
  - o Jews chose their leader and mainly followed their own laws

- Golden age of Jewish culture in Spain (950-1150)
  - Jewish scholars forge ahead in science, math, philosophy, and theology
  - Sephardic and Ashkenazi Jews
  - Rashi's commentary
- Almohad Caliphate outlaws Judaism and Christianity in southern Spain
- Muslim Seljuk Turks capture Jerusalem in 1071

Chapter 6: Medieval Judaism II: Crusades and the Mamluk Period

The Muslim Seljuk Turks not only captured Jerusalem in 1071 but also the Byzantine emperor Romanos IV Diogenes in Anatolia (western Turkey). The Byzantines had fought fiercely for their territory in western Turkey and suffered a crushing loss. The Turkish Sultan Alp Arslan sent Romanos back to Constantinople after the emperor promised to pay a ransom of 1.5 million gold pieces and give his daughter in marriage to the sultan's son. But Romanos returned home to a coup led by the Doukas family, who blinded their emperor and usurped power.

The Byzantine Empire spent the next few years in the chaos of unstable leadership, in no position to regain its territory in Asia. Nor could they do anything about Jerusalem, which wasn't a priority anyway. Several Muslim caliphates had held Jerusalem for the past four centuries, yet they allowed pilgrims to visit and permitted Christians and Jews to live there with certain restrictions.

The Byzantines wanted all of Anatolia back. Their capital Constantinople sat on the Bosphorus Strait that divided Europe from Asia and formed a channel between the Black Sea and the Aegean. As long as they controlled both sides of the strait, they controlled the lucrative sea trade. But now, the Seljuk Turks held territory just a few miles from the channel, far too close for comfort, and had nearly wiped out the Byzantine army.

Emperor Alexius Comnenus hoped to enlist aid from Western Europe, which was staging a comeback from its cultural and economic Dark Ages. He contacted Pope Urban II for help in driving out the Turks. It had been forty years since the Great Schism divided the Roman Catholic Church from the Eastern Orthodox Church. The pope liked the idea of the two sides fighting together for a common cause in what he hoped would be the first step toward reunification. So, he rebuked Europe's Christian states for fighting each other when they needed to fight together to free Jerusalem. He embellished stories of atrocities the Muslims had committed against Christians in the Holy Land and promised remission of sins for anyone who died fighting the infidel Turks.

In 1095, the Crusaders rallied in France and Germany. Some believed that before marching to Jerusalem to fight the Muslim infidels, they needed to deal with the Jewish infidels at home. Godfrey of Bouillon, one of the leaders of the First Crusade, swore that before leaving, he would avenge Christ's blood by eradicating all Jews in France. Other medieval Europeans recommended that all the Jews either convert or be killed and their property seized.

A 1234 CE illustration of violence against Jews
https://commons.wikimedia.org/wiki/File:Execution_of_Hebrews_by_Pagans.jpg

In the summer of 1095, frenzied mobs of French and German peasants attacked the Jewish communities in the Rhineland, massacring thousands. In Regensburg, Bavaria, a mob rounded up the Jewish community, forcing them into the Danube River in an involuntary baptism. Count Emicho led ten thousand of crusaders through Germany's Rhine Valley the following summer. Despite the Holy Roman Emperor Henry IV's orders to protect the Jews, Emicho's army killed at least 800 Jews in Worms and 1,100 in Mainz who refused Christian baptism.[50]

Meanwhile, waves of professional armies and ordinary citizens marched toward Constantinople on the way to Jerusalem. An estimated 100,000 Crusaders crossed the Bosphorus Strait into Asia, recapturing Nicaea and Edessa in Anatolia and Antioch in Syria. The Crusaders reached Jerusalem in 1099 and laid siege to the city, led by Godfrey of Bouillon. The Christians in Jerusalem had been sent away before the Crusaders arrived, as the Muslims feared they would fight on the Crusaders' side. But the Jews fought alongside the Muslims to defend their ancient city.

A fifty-foot-high defensive wall surrounded Jerusalem, but the Crusaders used two siege towers on wheels, a battering ram, and ladders to scale the wall. The Europeans broke into the city on July 15, 1099, after a five-week siege. The Crusaders dashed through the streets, killing tens of thousands of Muslims and Jews until blood reached the knees of their horses. Many Jews hid in their central synagogue, which the Crusaders burned down over their heads.[51]

---

[50] Iris Shagrir and Netta Amir, "The Persecution of the Jews in the First Crusade: Liturgy, Memory, and Nineteenth-Century Visual Culture," *Speculum* 92, no. 2 (2017): 405–28. http://www.jstor.org/stable/26340194.

[51] H. A. R. Gibb, *The Damascus Chronicle of the Crusades: Extracted and Translated from the Chronicle of Ibn Al-Qalanisi* (Mineola, New York: Dover Publications, 2003), 48.

Crusaders Take Jerusalem 1099, by Émile Signol
Photo zoomed in. Public Domain:
https://commons.wikimedia.org/wiki/File:Taking_of_Jerusalem_by_the_Crusaders,_15th_July_1099.jpg

Other Jews fled to the Temple Mount, where thousands of Muslims had taken refuge in the Dome of the Rock or the Al-Aqsa Mosque. The Crusaders slaughtered ten thousand men, women, and children on the Temple Mount. The stench of corpses filled the city, and the Europeans ordered the survivors to drag the bodies outside the city gates, where they were piled into pyramid-like stacks to be burned. Jerusalem remained in the hands of Christian rulers for almost a century. As historian Salo Baron states:

> "In many ways, 1096 marked a turning point in Jewish history. The trail of blood and smoldering ruins left behind in the Jewish communities from France to Palestine...for the first time brought home to the Jewish people, its foes and friends, the utter instability of the Jewish position in the western world...from the First Crusade on, anti-Jewish persecutions exercised a dangerously contagious appeal, which in periods of great emotional stress degenerated into mass

psychosis transcending national boundaries."⁵²

Judah Halevi was a Jewish biblical scholar and poet who lived in Cordoba, Spain, during the First Crusade. He also studied metaphysics, philosophy, and science, but his most outstanding contributions were his nationalistic poems and liturgy for synagogue worship. As his people suffered from violent mobs triggered by the Crusades, his poetry and songs alluded to Zionism: the return of Jews to Israel with Jewish statehood.

In 1144, the Seljuks recaptured Edessa and killed or enslaved the European Christians but spared the Turkish and Syrian Christians. Fears of the Turks retaking Jerusalem sparked the Second Crusade in 1146, fanned by the preaching of Bernard of Clairvaux. A French monk named Radulphe declared that the Jews deserved to die because they were enemies of Christianity, once again spurring violence against the Jews of Germany, Bohemia, and France. Two archbishops gave the Jews shelter in their castles, but a mob stormed one of the castles and killed the Jews in front of the Archbishop of Mainz.

The Second Crusade was a fiasco for the Europeans in the Middle East. King Conrad III of Germany and King Louis VII of France failed to retake Edessa. The Europeans were disorganized, and the Muslim forces were better trained and equipped. Forty years later, Jerusalem fell to Saladin, a Sunni Muslim sultan of Syria and Egypt. Saladin allowed the Jews to resettle in Jerusalem; many moved there from Ashkelon on the coast.

With the Muslims holding Jerusalem again, Pope Leo III called for the Third Crusade, which launched in 1189. This Crusade impacted England's Jews, most of whom had arrived in 1066 from Normandy with William the Conqueror. Once again, the Crusade rhetoric stirred up anti-Semitic actions. For instance, Jews in London were taxed one-quarter of their moveable property in 1188, and the crowds attacked Jews attending Richard the Lionheart's coronation in 1189. In York, a group of Jews hid in Clifford's Tower from a rampaging mob, but over 150 ultimately committed mass suicide as they realized the hopelessness of survival.

---

⁵² Salo W. Baron, *A Social and Religious History of the Jews* (New York: Columbia University Press, 1957), Vol. 4:89.

The Holy Roman Emperor Frederick I Barbarossa was the first to lead his troops to Asia on the Third Crusade in 1190, but he drowned when crossing a river in Turkey. King Richard the Lionheart of England and King Philip II of France sailed to the Middle East in 1191. They won a battle against Saladin at the northern Israeli city of Acre, where they captured three thousand Muslim prisoners. Saladin also held some Christian prisoners. The terms of surrender included each side releasing their prisoners, with Saladin agreeing to pay a hefty ransom for his men.

While negotiations continued, Richard and Philip had a falling out, and Philip sailed back to France with his men. Saladin released some of his prisoners but delayed releasing the rest. Richard lost his patience and marched 2,700 of his Muslim prisoners in front of Acre's walls, then cut their heads off. Saladin retaliated by killing the remainder of his English and French prisoners.

Saladin continued to fight Richard for another year around the land of Palestine, but without Philip's French army, Richard could not prevail. Eventually, they made a truce. King Richard got a strip of coastline from Jaffa to Tyre, and Saladin kept Jerusalem. Saladin allowed the Jerusalem Jews to stay and let Christian pilgrims visit Jerusalem's holy sites. In 1210, three hundred rabbis from France and England made *aliyah* (ascent to the Holy Land) and resettled in Palestine.

As in earlier times, some Muslim rulers had forced Jews (and Christians) to wear distinguishing clothing items, such as a yellow star, belt, or hood (Christians wore blue). In 1215, the Roman Catholic Church decreed that Jews had to wear a badge or pointed hat. The theologian Thomas Aquinas even called for the enslavement of all Jews. In 1229, King Henry III taxed the Jews of England 50 percent of their property's value.

Goaded by the Inquisition, on the Sabbath day of March 3, 1240, French officials seized every copy of the Talmud they could find in France. Twenty-four wagon loads hauled the parchments to Paris, where they were burned. In 1254, King Louis IX expelled all Jews from France, and King Edward I did the same in England in 1290. When Germany, Spain, and Italy followed suit, these expulsions created an eastward migration of Jews to Central and Eastern Europe, especially Poland.

Beginning in the 9th century, the Muslims captured teen boys from the Eurasian Steppe, converted them to Islam, and trained them for military service. Known as Mamluks (slaves), these rugged youths had acquired exceptional archery and horsemanship skills before being enslaved. Combined with the Muslim military training, the Mamluks were fierce and indomitable mounted archers, striking fear in anyone fighting against them. The Mamluks played a pivotal role in fighting with Saladin against the Crusaders.

Over time, the Mamluks grew in power despite technically being slaves, attaining high positions in the military. In 1250, the Mamluks took the throne in Egypt in the chaos following the Egyptian sultan's death. Ten years later, they hammered the Mongols swarming northern Palestine and conquered Syria as far north as the Euphrates River. The fourth Mamluk sultan of Egypt was Baybars I. While warring against the Crusaders and Mongols, he also organized the state, reformed its legal system, and enlarged the army. He conquered Acre in 1291, which the Crusaders had held since Richard the Lionheart had captured it a century earlier.

Mamluk warrior
https://commons.wikimedia.org/wiki/File:Mamluke.jpg

Although Christians and Jews were "protected people" under Muslim law, the Mamluks were nervous about the high administrative positions some of them held. Would they be more loyal to the Crusaders or Egypt? The Mamluks began strongly encouraging conversion to Islam, especially among the Coptic Christians who handled taxes and other financial affairs. The Mamluks sometimes swept the Jews into their conversion efforts. Those who refused to convert lost their positions. Rather than convert, many Egyptian Christians and a few Egyptian Jews left the country.

Riots erupted in Cairo against Christians in 1293, and Sultan Malik al-Ashraf Khalil dismissed all Jews and Christians from administrative positions. In 1301, more riots broke out, this time involving both Jews and Christians, forcing them to convert to Islam and closing all of Cairo's synagogues and churches. Jews had to wear yellow turbans and Christians blue turbans.

Originating in northern Asia, the Black Plague swept the Mediterranean coast from 1347 to 1349. Spreading to Europe, it killed about half the population. The plague and its ramifications plunged Egypt's economy into disarray, inciting more angst against non-Muslims. Rioters grabbed Jews and Christians and threw them into fires if they refused to recite the Shahada (the Muslim creed). The Jews were also suffering financially. They had once enjoyed a middle-class status in Egypt, and some were wealthy. The sultanate itself suffered economically due to the plague and other factors. Now, Jews in higher positions had lost their jobs, and most Jews were struggling through poverty.

In 1442, the Egyptian authorities found what they considered blasphemous writing against Islam in a Jewish synagogue. The name "Muhammed" was faintly inscribed on a raised platform upon which the rabbi would stand to read the scriptures; thus, he was "standing on Muhammed." The Mamluks destroyed the platform, then inspected other synagogues and churches. They discussed cutting off the feet or hands of the rabbis who had stood on Muhammed's name, but the rabbis vehemently denied knowing it was there. Under torture, three rabbis confessed. Two died, and the third converted to Islam.

Inspecting other synagogues and churches revealed that some had built new structures against the Pact of Umar. Others had renovated their interiors following a fire. Despite the Jews and Christians showing certificates of approval from the authorities for the renovations, the

Mamluks insisted they were breaking the pact made in 632 in Jerusalem. Many of the Jews and Christians were unaware of the ancient pact, so they were all informed of its contents and warned that any further infractions would result in the destruction of their synagogue or church.[53]

Although Jews were harassed under Mamluk rule, their plight paled compared to what happened to Jews in Europe. Blaming the Black Plague on Jews poisoning the wells, European mobs destroyed hundreds of Jewish communities. An anti-Semitic campaign in Barcelona, Castille, and Valencia killed thousands of Jews in 1391. Pope Benedict XIII banned the Talmud in 1415, and Jews were forced to live in ghettos throughout Europe.

Key Takeaways:
- The Crusades (1095-1291)
  - Byzantine Empire enlists the pope's aid in expelling Seljuk Turks
  - Crusade rhetoric spurs violence against Jews in France, Bohemia, and Spain
  - Crusaders take Jerusalem in 1099, with horrific atrocities against Jews and Muslims
  - Saladin, sultan of Syria and Egypt, retakes Jerusalem in 1187, allowed Jews to return
  - Third Crusade: Saladin keeps Jerusalem, and Jews are able to remain
- Jewish persecution and exile in Western Europe create an eastern migration
- The Mamluk period (1250-1517)
  - Former slaves who rose to power as Egypt's military force
  - Jews and Christians persecuted, although not as severely as in Western Europe

---

[53] Mark R. Cohen, "Jews in the Mamlūk Environment: The Crisis of 1442 (A Geniza Study)," *Bulletin of the School of Oriental and African Studies, University of London* 47, no. 3 (1984): 425–48. http://www.jstor.org/stable/618879.

Chapter 7: The Holocaust

The Nazis' "Final Solution to the Jewish Question" between 1941 and 1945 was the concluding stage in their evolving anti-Semitic policies. The original plan was to segregate the Jews, take their property, and ship them somewhere else, like Madagascar. The "final solution" was the systematic genocide of all Jews in Europe. How did things reach this point? What events and underlying philosophies led to an organized attempt to annihilate the Jewish race?

A century earlier, circumstances were gradually improving for the European Jews as the countries moved toward granting Jews citizenship and civil rights. By the mid-1800s, the Jews in all of Germany except Bavaria had equal rights with the rest of the population, at least on paper. The Jewish lawyer Gabriel Riesser even became vice-president of Germany's National Assembly in 1848.

Yet many Germans equated the Jews with modernity and the leftist Progressive Party, which they believed threatened traditional German values. University professors and clergymen fanned into flame this animosity toward the Jews. In 1878, the court chaplain Adolf Stoecker founded the German Christian Social Party, demanding that all Jews convert to Christianity and calling them "parasites" and a "nation unto themselves."

Kaiser Wilhelm II became Germany's last emperor in 1888 and ruled until his abdication in 1918. He had several personal friends who were Jews and supported the Zionist movement, albeit with racist reasons: he preferred they not live in Germany. Yet, over time, his attitude degenerated into "eliminatory" anti-Semitism. By the end of his life, he called for the extinction of the Jewish race:

> "They keep my people poor and in their clutches. In every small village in Germany sits a dirty Jew, like a spider drawing the people into the web of usury. He lends money to the small farmers on the security of their land and so gradually acquires control of everything. The Jews are the parasites of my empire. The Jewish question is one of the great problems I have to deal with, and yet nothing can be done to cope with it!"[54]

Meanwhile, by 1866, Jews had become Jerusalem's majority population and built a suburb outside the walls to eliminate overcrowding. Following horrific pogroms (organized massacres) in Russia, the First *Aliyah* brought almost 35,000 Jews to Palestine from 1882 to 1903. Their goal was "the political, national, and spiritual resurrection of the Jewish people in Palestine"[55] under the patronage of Baron Edmond de Rothschild of France.

Photo from the 1930s of **Degania**, Israel's first kibbutz

Photo zoomed in. Credit: קיבוץ דגניה א, CC BY-SA 3.0 <https://creativecommons.org/licenses/by-sa/3.0>, via Wikimedia Commons;
https://commons.wikimedia.org/wiki/File:Historical_Image_of_Degania_Elementary_School_(9).png

---

[54] John C. G. Rohl, *The Kaiser and His Court: Wilhelm II and the Government of Germany* (Cambridge: Cambridge University Press,1995), 190-212.

[55] "Immigration to Israel: The First Aliyah (1882-1903)," *Jewish Virtual Library* https://www.jewishvirtuallibrary.org/the-first-aliyah-1882-1903

Following Russia's October Revolution led by Vladimir Lenin's Bolshevik Party, Jews fleeing Marxist anti-Semitism formed the Second Aliyah in 1904. In 1906, the Jews founded the first Hebrew high school in Jaffa and the Bezalel Academy of Art and Design in Jerusalem. In 1909, the Jews built Tel Aviv just outside the port city of Jaffa as a housing estate for Hebrew-speaking Jews. Zionist pioneers established Degania Alef in 1910, the first kibbutz (a farming commune) south of the Sea of Galilee.

World War I raged from 1914 to 1919, with the Allies (France, Italy, Japan, Russia, the United Kingdom, and the United States) pitted against the Central Powers (Austria-Hungary, Bulgaria, Germany, and the Ottoman Empire). Although 100,000 Jews fought for Germany, they were unjustly accused of evading active service. The British seized Palestine from the Ottoman Empire and announced their plan of establishing a "national home for the Jewish people" in the Balfour Declaration of 1917.

From 1919 to 1923, the Third Aliyah of 40,000 young Eastern European Jews increased Palestine's Jewish population to 90,000 pioneers building roads and towns around Palestine. The Fourth Aliyah of 1924 to 1929 brought 82,000 middle-class Jews from Poland, who established factories and small businesses. The European Jews not only built up Palestine's infrastructure and economy but also higher education. The Hebrew University of Jerusalem opened in 1925. When Hitler became Germany's chancellor in 1933, 250,000 German Jewish professionals fled to Palestine in the Fifth Aliyah. They established industrial enterprises and built the Haifa port and oil refineries. Almost a half-million Jews lived in Palestine by 1939.

As a young man, Adolf Hitler nurtured a pathological loathing of Marxists and Jews. He blamed the Jews for Germany's cultural, economic, and political chaos, proclaiming they were corrupting Germany and the "Aryan" race. Just before the end of World War I, he was blinded after being gassed and spent months in recovery, where he gradually regained his eyesight. He spent that time seething about losing the war and fantasizing about rescuing Germany and Austria from the Jews and Bolsheviks (Russian Marxists).

Hitler joined the Workers' Party and became its chairman in 1921. Although of average height and dark-haired, Hitler advanced the ideal image of tall, muscular blonds with blue or green eyes. Hitler gave dramatic and fiery speeches that the "Aryan" Germans were a master race and that the Jews were the cause of Germany's domestic issues. He announced the "Platform of the National-Socialist German Workers' Party," demanding all ethnic Germans unify into one "Reich," or "Greater Germany." Only those of German blood could be citizens; all Jews were explicitly excluded. The platform stated that the Party "fights against the Jewish-materialistic spirit within and around us."[56]

At this point, Hitler talked about removing Jews' privileges and exiling them, not exterminating them. An unsuccessful coup d'état in 1923 landed him in prison for nine months. He used that time to write *Mein Kampf* (*My Struggle*), outlining his ideas about the Aryan race, the Jewish threat, social Darwinism, and his plan of *Lebensraum* (living space)—his concept of conquering all of Europe and deporting non-German people to Siberia so people of German blood could spread out and multiply.

After their humiliating defeat in World War I, which crippled their economy, many Germans were susceptible to Hitler's propaganda. The Great Depression crushed Germany's economy even further, bringing people of all classes, including industrialists and military leaders, into the Nazi Party. By 1932, the Nazis controlled the parliament, and Hitler became Germany's Reich Chancellor in 1933.

Hitler immediately eliminated the Jews, Marxists, and Social Democrats from any political role. Within two months, he established Dachau, Germany's first concentration camp for political prisoners. These prisoners had no indictment or conviction of any crime; the judicial system wasn't followed. This first concentration camp was meant to silence and intimidate anyone considered a threat to the Reich.

---

[56] "The Program of the National-Socialist German Workers' Party, February 24, 1920," *Jewish Virtual Library* https://www.jewishvirtuallibrary.org/platform-of-the-national-socialist-german-workers-rsquo-party

Dachau concentration camp after liberation by the US Army on April 29, 1945. A Russian prisoner points to a guard who brutally mistreated prisoners.
https://commons.wikimedia.org/wiki/File:Konzentrationslager_Dachau_1945.webp

By 1934, Hitler was the unchallenged leader of the "Third Reich"— the third German empire. As he successfully rejuvenated Germany's military and economy, the Germans were so giddy at their comeback that most were unconcerned about the Nuremberg Laws of 1935. These laws stripped Jews of citizenship, which meant Jews lost their jobs in civil service. Even physicians and teachers were forced into unemployment when the hospitals and schools fell under government regulation. The Jews who emigrated had to pay a 90 percent tax on their assets.

In April 1934, Heinrich Himmler took command of the Berlin Gestapo (the secret state police) and the concentration camps. With meticulous methodology, he organized systematic terrorism against the regime's opponents. Himmler and Hitler broadened the criteria for the concentration camps to anyone they deemed inferior. People with hydrocephaly, deformities, Jewish ancestry, and anything else considered "subhuman" were herded into the camps.

On November 9-10, 1938, Hitler coordinated violence against Jews in Kristallnacht: "the night of broken glass." Mobs that included Nazi soldiers and Hitler Youth disguised in civilian clothing plundered and burned Jewish homes, businesses, and synagogues in Germany, Austria, and Czechoslovakia. Firefighters intervened only to preserve neighboring properties. The police arrested 30,000 young male Jews, sending them to the Dachau, Sachsenhausen, and Buchenwald concentration camps.

World War II launched on September 1, 1939, when Hitler invaded Poland. He used *blitzkrieg* tactics: shock assaults with bombers and fighter planes to immobilize military bases, airfields, and communication centers, followed by infantry invasion. Poland fell within a month, then Norway, Denmark, Holland, Belgium, Luxemburg, and France in rapid succession. All of Western Europe except Great Britain fell to the Nazis within nine months.

As the war began, Hitler initiated his T-4 Euthanasia Program, rounding up men, women, and children with psychological illnesses and those mentally and physically disabled. At the killing centers of Bernburg, Brandenburg, Grafeneck, Hadamar, and Hartheim, the Nazis murdered the children with sedatives and the adults by starvation. Later, they began gassing the victims. The Germans also used the concentration camps for forced labor in manufacturing military equipment and artificial rubber. These prisoners lived an average of nine months due to insufficient food, backbreaking work, and overcrowding leading to typhus and other diseases.

An emaciated teenage boy rescued from the Ebensee concentration camp
Photo zoomed in. Credit: J Malan Heslop, colorized by Julius Jääskeläinen, CC BY 2.0 <https://creativecommons.org/licenses/by/2.0>, via Wikimedia Commons; https://commons.wikimedia.org/wiki/File:Liberated_prisoner_of_the_Ebensee_concentration_camp_in_Austria,_8_May_1945._(45899003575).jpg

On the war front, the British Air Force held off Nazi control of the English Channel, so Hitler turned his military machine against Eastern Europe and North Africa. He took Greece, Yugoslavia, and Crete and invaded the Soviet Union in June 1941. Although Hitler's armies overwhelmed the Communist forces in the Baltic States and Ukraine, he overextended his military. He was unable to conquer Moscow before the deadly Russian winter set in.

In December, the United States joined the war on the side of Britain and the Soviet Union, the Allied powers, which Hitler called "international Jewry." Earlier, the Nazis had planned to exile one million Jews to Nazi-run Madagascar each year for four years. However, the British blockade kept that from happening, so Hitler resorted to his "Final Solution to the Jewish Question," the mass murder of all Jews under Nazi rule.

In Russia, Hitler shot or starved to death over three million POWs: Communists, intellectuals, and Jews. In September 1941, Himmler masterminded the Babi Yar massacre. The Nazis posted notices in Kyiv, instructing all Jews to report to the Babi Yar ravine with warm clothing, documentation, and valuables. Since Babi Yar was close to the train station, the Jews assumed they would be evacuated by train, and over 33,000 gathered in the early morning. To their horror, all the men, women, and children were stripped, forced into the ravine, and shot.

Because of the anguish the German soldiers experienced in shooting women and children, Himmler decided to use "gas vans." Jews, Gypsies, and mentally ill people were herded into the back of sealed trucks, believing they were being transported somewhere. Instead, the engine exhaust was diverted into the back of the truck, killing the people. In 1941, gas "showers" were installed in Poland's Belzec, Sobibor, and Treblinka concentration camps.

As unsuspecting people were unloaded from cattle cars on the trains arriving at the camps, the elderly, children, pregnant women, and anyone too sick or weak to work were divided off. They were told they needed a "disinfecting" shower but instead died from carbon monoxide gas piped into the shower room. Himmler organized the murder of almost 2.7 million Jews, Gypsies, homosexuals, political prisoners, and social misfits at the concentration camps.

At the Auschwitz concentration camp in Poland, Nazi scientists conducted experiments with Zyklon B, a poisonous insecticide and rat killer, on Soviet prisoners of war. Zyklon B became the preferred gassing method at Auschwitz for its swift and efficient action. Five hundred Jews were herded into the "showers" daily to be gassed. On October 10, 1944, the Nazis gassed eight hundred children at Auschwitz.

Hungarian Jews who have just deboarded the train at Auschwitz concentration camp. The healthy are separated out for labor. The old lady in the center front and the lady holding the baby were probably immediately sent to the gas chambers.
https://commons.wikimedia.org/wiki/File:Selection_on_the_ramp_at_Auschwitz-Birkenau,_1944_(Auschwitz_Album)_1b.jpg

When the Jews and other prisoners first arrived at Auschwitz, those who weren't immediately gassed were designated for the labor force. The guards shaved their heads, tattooed their arms with a registration number, and issued striped uniforms. They lived in overcrowded dormitories with tiers of bunks. In the following months, a physician would determine who was still healthy enough to work and who would be sent to the gas chambers. The prisoners who worked at the gas chambers later shared that amid the screams, they could hear the Sh'ma Yisrael: "Hear, oh Israel, the L-rd is our G-d, the L-rd is One."

Those in concentration camps who weren't gassed sometimes faced worse horrors. To keep the Jews from producing more children, physicians irradiated the reproductive systems of men and women or injected chemicals that burned the women's uteruses. Nazi doctors infected prisoners with diseases to test new medications, and some prisoners were frozen to experiment with hyperthermia treatments.

The tide began to turn in 1943 as the Nazis lost North Africa and Sicily to the Allies. The Allies took Italy and Normandy in June 1944, sandwiching the German forces between them and Soviet troops. The Soviet forces liberated the prisoners of the Majdanek concentration camp in Poland that summer, sharing evidence of the slaughters committed there with journalists. The Soviets released six thousand starving prisoners at Auschwitz in January 1945. The Nazis had already left weeks earlier, forcing most of the prisoners on a death march. As the Allied forces continued to liberate the camps, they found unspeakable horrors. Unburied corpses were stacked like firewood. The survivors had lost their body fat and muscle and were skin and bones.

The German army unraveled as its generals seethed under Hitler's distrustful and deranged leadership. A failed assassination attempt on Hitler ended in the generals' gruesome executions, filmed for Hitler's pleasure. As the Allies approached Berlin, Hitler studied his maps and ordered attacks with armies he didn't have. On April 30, 1945, Hitler committed suicide, and the German Third Reich surrendered on May 7, 1945. World War II ended on September 2, 1945, after Japan's surrender.

Two-thirds of the European Jews died in the Holocaust—about six million. Poland had three million Jews in 1933; the Holocaust reduced that number to 45,000. Greece lost 90 percent of its Jewish population. Most survivors emigrated to Palestine, the United States, Australia, or South Africa. By 1950, over half the world's Jewish population lived in the western hemisphere.

For the Jewish survivors, it was time to pick up the pieces of their shattered lives and forge ahead with the tenacity that carried them through the unimaginable nightmare of the Holocaust. However, anti-Semitism did not die with the Nazi regime. The Jews were still not safe in Europe; over five hundred Jews were killed in Poland in the year after liberation by their former neighbors or roving gangs. Would it ever be possible to live normal lives again? And where would that be?

Women in the Auschwitz barracks
https://commons.wikimedia.org/wiki/File:Women_in_the_barracks_of_Auschwitz.jpg

Key Takeaways:

- Circumstances for Jews in the century before the Holocaust
  - Citizenship and civil rights in most European countries
  - Antisemitic attitudes continue; Jews blamed for economic woes
- Jews resettle in Palestine
  - The majority population in Jerusalem by 1866
  - One-half million Jews settle in Palestine from 1882 to 1933
  - Build Tel Aviv, universities, schools, roads, farms, the first kibbutz
  - 1917 British Balfour Declaration: a "national home for the Jewish people"
- Hitler becomes Germany's Reich Chancellor in 1933
  - Establishes Dachau, Germany's first concentration camp, in 1933
  - Nuremberg Laws of 1935 strip Jews of citizenship
  - In 1938, Hitler coordinates violence against Jews in Kristallnacht

- World War II launches on September 1, 1939, when Hitler invades Poland
    - All of Western Europe except Britain falls to the Nazis in nine months
    - Most Jews forced into concentration camps to work or die
- In 1941, Operation Reinhard initiated to kill all Jews in Europe
    - Babi Yar massacre: 33,000 Jewish men, women, and children shot in Kiev
    - Gas vans and gas chambers kill over one million Jews
    - Eight hundred children gassed in one day at Auschwitz
- Allied forces gain the upper hand in the war in 1944
    - Soviets begin liberating Jews from some of the concentration camps
    - 1945: Hitler commits suicide, Third Reich surrenders, war ends
- Impact of the Holocaust on Jews in Europe
    - Two-thirds of European Jews killed: six million
    - Most survivors emigrate to Palestine, the United States, Australia, or South Africa
    - Antisemitic violence continues to kill Jews in Europe

Chapter 8: Modern Israel

Immediately after WWII, while the Allied administration was still in place, about 250,000 Jews lived in Germany. Some were married to German spouses and had escaped notice during the Nazi regime. Others were children sheltered by kindhearted German neighbors pretending they were their own, saved from being dragged with their parents to concentration camps. A third group was German Jews who had returned from exile.

The fourth and largest group was the thousands of Jews who had survived the "death marches" to Germany from Eastern European concentration camps in the war's final weeks. After "liberation," three-quarters of the Jews in Germany still lived in the overcrowded camps, fighting typhus and typhoid fever while the Allies debated what to do with them. Eighty percent were from Poland; the rest were from Russia, Romania, Hungary, and Czechoslovakia.

When General Patton wanted to transport them back to where they came from, they refused. Their Eastern European communities had been wiped out, and their property confiscated. They had no family, no homes, and no employment there. Pogroms (organized massacres) against Jews were ongoing in Poland, and Jews in the Soviet bloc quickly discovered that Stalin's boast of eliminating anti-Semitism was fiction.[57]

---

[57] Michael Brenner, *After the Holocaust: Rebuilding Jewish Lives in Postwar Germany*, trans. Barbara Harshav. (Princeton: Princeton University Press, 1997), 3-16.

The inmates demanded to be sent to Palestine, where a thriving Jewish community comprised about 30 percent of the population. Jews throughout Europe echoed the demands of the Jews in Germany. They needed a place of safety to heal and rebuild their lives. They needed to recover the culture that defined them: their religious observances, the Yiddish and Hebrew languages, traditions, music, art, and literature.

The Jews in the "displaced persons" camps initiated a renaissance of Jewish culture, launching newspapers, Jewish schools, and historical committees between 1945 and 1951. They published papers in Yiddish, Hebrew, Polish, German, Hungarian, Lithuanian, and Romanian with printing presses brought into the camps.[58] They shared their stories, angst, and dreams through the written word in their own languages, giving the European Jews a united voice.

Jewish Youth in the Fifth Aliyah to Palestine, February 19, 1934
Zoltan Kluger, Public Domain: https://commons.wikimedia.org/wiki/File:First_Youth-Aliyah_group_walking_to_Ein_Harod.JPG

But was Palestine a viable option for Jewish resettlement? A Jewish remnant had lived there through the Greek, Roman, Christian, and Muslim occupations. And, since the 1880s, Jews had moved back to Palestine in increasing numbers. Other Palestinians had a much longer history in the land. About 70 percent of Palestine's population in 1946

---

[58] Brenner, *After the Holocaust*, 16-19.

was non-Jewish, primarily Muslim Arabs whose forefathers came in the centuries after Caliph Umar invaded Palestine in 638 CE.

Recent genetic studies have revealed that Jews and Palestinians are related, sharing 18 percent of their chromosomes. Both have high repeat numbers of DYS388 alleles and share a single branch in Haplogroup 1. Geneticists believe this link extends back to the Roman era or earlier and think it remarkable that the two groups maintained genetic continuity even though most Jews had lived outside Israel for two thousand years.[59] Some Palestinians report a family history of Jewish ancestors who converted to Islam, while others claim to be descendants of the ancient Canaanites.

Despite their shared ancestry, the Jews and Palestinians were divided by religion and culture. The Palestinians regarded the Jews as recent intruders in their homeland. At the end of WWI in 1918, the Allies had assigned Palestine to Great Britain in the British Mandate of 1920. The mandate incorporated the Balfour Declaration supporting Palestine as a national home for the Jewish people.

The Palestinians demanded independence from British rule and an end to Jewish immigration, as the Jews and Palestinians violently clashed over their claims to the land. The British turned the problem over to the United Nations in 1947. The UN proposed ending the British Mandate for Palestine and establishing separate Palestinian and Jewish states in the land, with Jerusalem under an International Trusteeship.

---

[59] Almut Nebel et al, "High-resolution Y Chromosome Haplotypes of Israeli and Palestinian Arabs Reveal Geographic Substructure and Substantial Overlap with Haplotypes of Jews," *Human Genetics* 107, no. 6 (December 2000): 630–641. doi:10.1007/s004390000426.

In 1947, the United Nations Partition Plan had the Arabs in the light areas, the Jews in the dark areas, and Jerusalem under UN control.
https://commons.wikimedia.org/wiki/File:UN_Partition_Plan_For_Palestine_1947.png

The British Mandate for Palestine ended on May 14, 1948, and David Ben Gurion, Israel's first prime minister, declared Israel an independent and democratic state. He proclaimed Israel was the Jewish historical and spiritual homeland, but its Arab citizens would have equal and nondiscriminatory treatment. On the same day, the Israel Defense Forces (IDF) were formally established from underground forces already in operation.

The next day, five Arab nations (Egypt, Lebanon, Iraq, Transjordan, and Syria) invaded the new nation of Israel, declaring, "It will be a war of annihilation." Israel's War of Independence raged from May 1948 to July 1949. Jerusalem's "Old City" (the part within the ancient walls) fell to the Arabs on May 30. For the first time in centuries, the Jews lost access to the Western Wall, the only remnant of the old temple.

However, Israel's tiny, fledgling air force stopped the Egyptian armored column invading from the south. By autumn, the Israeli Air Force achieved air superiority as seventeen bombers arrived from Czechoslovakia with experienced fighter pilots. Israel also had three ships the British had seized because they had been used to smuggle refugees from Europe. The Israelis snuck aboard the ships, sailed them to Tel Aviv, outfitted them with guns and anti-aircraft weaponry, and used them against Egypt.

Israel won the war in July 1949. It held the territory allotted by the United Nations and took 60 percent of the land assigned to the Palestinians. Israel made armistice agreements with Egypt, Jordan, Lebanon, and Syria, agreeing to the "Green Line," the new border between Israel and Palestine. Jordan now held the West Bank of the Jordan River, and Egypt had the Gaza Strip on the Mediterranean Sea.

About 700,000 displaced Palestinians moved into the West Bank, Gaza Strip, or surrounding Arab nations. Meanwhile, about 700,000 Jews moved into Israel from Arab countries that had expelled them and from Europe. On February 16, 1949, the Israelis elected their first Knesset (parliament), and the United Nations admitted Israel as its fifty-ninth member in May 1949.

Despite its armistice agreement with Israel, Egypt closed the Suez Canal to Israeli shipping. In 1951, the United Nations Security Council ordered Egypt to reopen the canal, insisting that a blockade was inconsistent with the armistice agreement. Egypt refused, and its foreign minister, Muhammad Salah al-Din, stated: "We shall not be satisfied except by the final obliteration of Israel from the map of the Middle East."

Egypt imported arms from the Soviet Union and sent *fedayeen* terrorists to attack Israel, mainly from Jordan's bases. Jordan bore the brunt of Israel's retaliation, and the Security Council chastised Israel for hostile acts. Egypt then nationalized the Suez Canal Company, which angered France and Britain. France had paid for 52 percent of the canal's construction in 1869, and Great Britain had purchased Egypt's shares in the Suez Canal Company in 1875.

France and Britain secretly plotted with Israel, and Israel invaded the Sinai Peninsula in 1956, advancing within ten miles of the canal. Several days later, Britain and France sent troops into the canal zone, which the United States condemned, considering it a continued act of European colonization.[60] The United Nations ordered Britain, France, and Israel to withdraw their troops from Egypt, and Egypt paid Britain and France for their shares in the Suez Canal Company.

In 1964, the Arab League formed the Palestinian Liberation Organization (PLO), eventually led by Yasser Arafat, who conducted terrorist operations against Israeli citizens. King Hussein of Jordan condemned the attacks for fear of Israeli retaliatory strikes on Jordan. King Hassan II of Morocco warned Israel that the Arab leaders were planning a war on Israel.

Meanwhile, Syria and Jordan were disturbed that Israel was draining water from the Sea of Galilee in its National Water Carrier canal that transported water to Israel's arid south, lowering water levels in the Jordan River that flows out of it and the Dead Sea, where it empties. Syria lay on Galilee's east bank, and Jordan lay on the eastern side of the Jordan River.

Syria began shelling Israeli villages and kibbutzim from the Golan Heights, a plateau towering three thousand feet over the eastern shores of the Sea of Galilee. Israel retaliated by shooting down six Syrian MiG fighters in 1967, so Syria called on Egypt for help. Egyptian forces lined up on Israel's Sinai border while Syrian troops amassed on the Golan

---

[60] "The Suez Crisis, 1956," *Office of the Historian. Foreign Service Institute: United States Department of State.* https://history.state.gov/milestones/1953-1960/suez#:~:text=On%20July%2026%2C%201956%2C%20Egyptian,since%20its%20constructio n%20in%201869.

Heights. Egypt cut off the Straits of Tiran, which flows from the Gulf of Aqaba at Israel's southern tip into the Red Sea. Losing ship traffic through the Straits of Tiran meant Israel couldn't import oil from Iran. Jordan, Lebanon, Iraq, Algeria, Kuwait, and Sudan allied with Egypt and Syria to wipe Israel off the map.

Using the element of surprise, Israel launched a preemptive strike on Egypt on June 5, 1967, flying almost its entire air force into Egypt and obliterating 180 fighter planes. Israel and Egypt then clashed in tank battles in the searing Sinai desert. Syria retaliated by attacking Tiberias and Megiddo, and Jordan shelled West Jerusalem. Israel's air force attacked the Syrian and Jordanian airfields, destroying half of Syria's air force and twenty Jordanian planes.

Three Israeli battalions headed to Jerusalem to rescue a small Jewish community in mostly-Arab East Jerusalem. They also needed to fend off the shelling attacks on West Jerusalem. The Israelis took the Jordanian command bunker in a brutal battle, but 249 of their 260 soldiers were wounded or killed. The Jordanians also suffered devastating losses.

The Israeli commanders decided to attack Jerusalem by the eastern Lion's Gate. (The only general to ever conquer Jerusalem from the east was King David when it was a Jebusite city.) Most Jordanian troops had evacuated the city, so the Jewish forces reached the Temple Mount unhindered. A rabbi blew the shofar at the Western Wall to celebrate. The Six-Day War ended with Israel gaining Jerusalem, tripling Israel's territory, and capturing the Sinai Peninsula.

But peace did not follow. Within three months, the Arab League formulated the "three no's": no peace, no negotiations, and no recognition of Israel as a nation. Egypt began shelling Israeli forces close to the Suez Canal, starting the War of Attrition. Using Soviet missiles, Egypt sank Israel's destroyer, the *Eilat*, in October 1967.

Israel had a small full-time military and depended on its reserve forces in wartime. (Even today, all able-bodied men serve in active duty for three years and then in the reserves until they are forty. All women do two years of active duty, and unmarried women without children serve in the reserves until they are thirty-eight. Women served in active combat in the War of Independence but, after that, filled non-combat roles until the 21st century.)

Egypt's President Nasser believed Israel could not sustain a lengthy war because its reserve forces would eventually need to return to their jobs. Israel's economy would crumble if the younger men and women were not manning the businesses, factories, and farms. Egypt was in this war for the long haul. The UN tried negotiating peace talks, but Egypt and Jordan refused to come to the table until Israel withdrew from the territory it gained in the Six-Day War.

Golda Meir and Richard Nixon at the White House, September 1969
https://commons.wikimedia.org/wiki/File:Golda_Meir_in_the_white_house_1969.jpg

Israel's new prime minister, Golda Meir, visited the United States, pledging Israel's willingness for armistice talks. President Nixon sent Secretary of State William Rogers to the Middle East to negotiate a ceasefire in 1970. The terms were that Israel would withdraw from the Sinai, Egypt would allow passage through the Strait of Tiran, and the two countries would commit to peace. The first ceasefire agreement fell through, but Rogers finally got Israel and Egypt to agree to an "in place" ceasefire in June 1970, maintaining the status quo regarding territory but ending the three-year war.

The following year, Egypt's new president, Anwar Sadat, hinted he would be open to recognizing Israel as a state if Israel returned the Sinai Peninsula and the Gaza Strip. Golda Meir signaled that Israel was willing to make some withdrawals, but *not* to where it was before the 1967 Six-Day War. In 1973, Sadat threatened to go to war against Israel, but he had been threatening for three years and had never done anything.

But then, Sadat suddenly did—on Yom Kippur, Israel's holiest day of the year. It was also Ramadan, Islam's most sacred festival. On October

6, 1973, Egypt and Syria launched a coordinated surprise assault, beginning the Yom Kippur War. At the Golan Heights, 1,400 Syrian tanks faced off against 180 Israeli tanks. At the Suez Canal, 2,000 Egyptian tanks, 550 Egyptian aircraft, and 600,000 Egyptian soldiers confronted 500 Israeli soldiers with three tanks.

Algeria, Iraq, Jordan, Kuwait, Lebanon, Libya, Morocco, Saudi Arabia, Sudan, and Tunisia supported Egypt and Syria with financing, fighter jets, soldiers, tanks, and radar units. Because the United States, Holland, Great Britain, Japan, and Portugal supported Israel, the Arabs imposed an oil embargo on these nations. Gas prices quadrupled, and President Nixon lowered the U.S. speed limit to fifty-five miles per hour to reduce fuel consumption.

After the Soviet Union transferred eight thousand tons of weapons to the Arabs, Nixon sent tanks, bombs, and helicopters to Israel. This influx enabled the Israeli forces to trounce the Egyptians in the Sinai, cross the Suez Canal, and march toward Cairo. In the north, the Israelis recaptured the Golan Heights and marched toward Syria's capital, Damascus. On October 22, the UN Security Council called for a ceasefire, and Israel complied under pressure from the US. Because President Sadat's initial attack was successful (until the US jumped in with weaponry), he felt that he had "retrieved Arab honor." He signed a peace treaty with Israel in 1979, and Israel returned the Sinai Peninsula to Egypt. Peace with Egypt endures today, over forty years later.

At an agonizingly slow pace, Israel and its Arab neighbors began to make peace. In 1994, the Israel-Jordan Peace Treaty was signed. In 2020, Israel normalized diplomatic ties with Bahrain, Morocco, Sudan, and the United Arab Emirates. In 2022, Israel formed a maritime deal with Lebanon, although the two countries technically remain at war. Syria and Iraq still do not recognize Israel as a legitimate state.

Peace between Israel and the Palestinians continues to be elusive and complicated. In 1993, Israel and the Palestinian Liberation Organization signed the Oslo Accords, giving the Palestinians interim self-government in Jericho and the Gaza Strip. A Palestinian Council was elected in 1995. In 1997, Israel signed the Hebron Protocol, promising to withdraw Israeli troops from Hebron and transfer power to the Palestinians.

In 2006, Hamas (Islamic Resistance Movement) was elected as the head of the Palestinian government. Hamas took the Gaza Strip from Fatah (formerly the Palestinian National Liberation Movement), dividing the Palestinians into the Hamas-led Gaza Strip and the Fatah-led West Bank in 2007. Hamas has refused negotiations with Israel while Fatah has been open. Both Hamas and Fatah want to rebuild a Palestinian state on the old 1967 borders.

What is the political makeup of the current State of Israel? It is a democratic state with freedom of the press and national elections every four years. Israel is a parliamentary republic with three separate governmental branches: the legislative (law-making), the executive (administrative), and the judiciary (judges and courts). The Knesset, or House of Representatives, is the legislative branch with 120 members.

The people of Israel vote for a party, not the individual president or prime minister. Each party receives a number of seats in the Knesset depending on how many votes they get. The Knesset elects Israel's president, who holds a ceremonial role in nominating a member of the Knesset for prime minister after consulting with party members. The candidate for prime minister has twenty-eight days to form a government platform. If the Knesset approves, he becomes prime minister, chief of the executive branch. The modern State of Israel celebrated its seventy-fifth year in 2023.

Key Takeaways:
- Rebuilding Jewish culture and civilization in the wake of the Second World War
    - Returning to former homes not an option: families, houses, and jobs gone
    - Jews in displacement camps launch newspapers and Jewish schools (1945-51)
- Establishment of Israel
    - British ends their control and establishes Jewish and Palestinian states
    - David Ben Gurion becomes prime minister of the new State of Israel in 1948
    - War of Independence May 1948-July 1949
- Conflicts in which Israel has been involved
    - Six-Day War, June 1967
    - War of Attrition with Egypt and Jordan, 1967-1970
    - Yom Kippur War, 1973

- Small steps toward peace in the Middle East
  - Enduring peace with Egypt after the Treaty of 1979
  - Israel makes peace with Jordan in 1994
  - Peace with Bahrain, Morocco, Sudan, and the United Arab Emirates in 2020
- Controversy over Palestine
  - 1993 Oslo Accords gives Palestinians self-government
  - 1997 Hebron Protocol: Israeli troops withdraw from Hebron
  - 2006: Hamas takes over Palestinians in Gaza Strip, Fatah takes over West Bank
- Current State of Israel
  - A democratic state with freedom of the press and national elections every four years
  - A parliamentary republic with legislative, executive, and judiciary branches
  - The legislative branch is the Knesset or House of Representatives, with 120 members
  - Israel's 75th birthday in 2023

Chapter 9: Customs, Traditions, Symbols, and Art

Some Jews are atheists, some are orthodox, and others are somewhere in between, yet the customs and traditions commemorating their shared history tie them together. As Jewish families celebrate Shabbat and the annual festivals, they absorb the essentials of Judaism's distinct culture. New customs, such as bar and bat mitzvahs, have emerged over the centuries and continue to define Judaism.

The Jewish dietary laws are called kosher (*kashrut*), which means "fitness." They are based on the Law of Moses given over three millennia ago in Devarim (Deuteronomy) 14:2-21 and Vayikra (Leviticus) 11. Some Jewish families keep kosher strictly, some only observe it at special times like the Passover (Pesach) week, some don't keep kosher at all, and some follow parts but not all the laws.

G-d permitted the Israelites to eat mammals with split hoofs that chewed cud: cattle, sheep, goats, and deer. Any animal without a divided hoof or that didn't chew its cud was forbidden; the Torah specifically mentions camels, rabbits, rock badgers, bats, and pigs as unclean animals. Jews could eat any marine animal with fins and scales; fish were fine, but not shellfish, eels, or dolphins. They could eat most birds except vultures and birds of prey. Flying insects could not be eaten unless they had leg joints, like grasshoppers or locusts. Crawling creatures like mice and lizards were forbidden. If the Israelites came across a dead animal, they could not eat it. Finally, they could not cook a baby goat in its mother's milk. This enigmatic command is repeated three times in the Torah.[61] Controversies arose over what this command meant. Maimonides (Moses ben Maimon) thought it referred to a pagan sacrificial ritual that the ancient Jews should avoid. In the Talmud, rabbis expanded Moses's law to say no meat of any kind could be cooked or served with dairy products.

Some rabbis forbade cooking meat in the same kitchen as dairy or mandated preparing them on separate countertops using separate dishes. Jews keeping strict kosher are not allowed cheeseburgers and lasagna because they mix meat and dairy. Some kosher Jews wait three hours between eating meat and dairy. Others will not eat yogurt or drink milk at the same table with someone eating meat.

The Torah teaches observing Shabbat (the Sabbath): "[For] six days, work may be performed, but on the seventh day, it is a complete rest day, a holy occasion; you shall not perform any work. It is a Sabbath to the L-rd in all your dwelling places."[62] G-d instituted the Sabbath from the time of creation as a blessed and sanctified day: "And G-d blessed the seventh day, and He hallowed it, for thereon He abstained from all His work that G-d created to do."[63]

Religious Jews keep Shabbat by resting from work from sunset on Friday until sundown on Saturday. On Friday, they clean their homes thoroughly, bathe, and put on nice clothes to celebrate this sacred day. At least eighteen minutes before sunset on Friday, the wife lights candles where the Shabbat meal will be enjoyed. A prayer of sanctification called *kiddush* is pronounced over the wine, and then everyone enjoys a delicious meal. On Saturday morning, faithful Jews attend Shabbat services, often followed by a light luncheon at their synagogue. Stringent observance of Shabbat among Orthodox Jews includes not driving on Saturday, not turning lights on and off, not using electrical appliances, and not cooking.

At Shabbat and most Jewish festivals (other than Passover), many wives (especially Ashkenazi Jews) prepare two loaves of braided challah bread. A small piece of the dough is separated and consecrated to G-d, following the Torah command in Bamidbar (Numbers) 15:20-21. After

---

[61] Shemot (Exodus) 23:19, 34:26, Devarim (Deuteronomy) 14:21

[62] Vayikra (Leviticus) 23:3

[63] Bereshit (Genesis) 2:2

the wine blessing, everyone washes their hands. Then the head of the household pronounces the *Hamotzi*: "Blessed are you L-RD our G-d, King of the Universe, who brings forth bread from the earth." Everyone eats the bread with salt, symbolizing G-d's eternal covenant with Israel.

Coming-of-age ceremonies are common for Jewish adolescent boys (bar mitzvah) and girls (bat mitzvah). This custom began in the Middle Ages. At a certain age, boys were expected to start participating in *mitzvot* (actions) in the synagogue, such as reading the Torah to the assembly or wearing *tefillin* (a leather case with Torah scriptures). Today, the bar and bat mitzvah ceremonies differ depending on whether the synagogue is Orthodox, Conservative, or Reformed. Usually, the boy or girl is called up to the platform to chant a passage from the Torah in Hebrew using cantillation and discuss its meaning. Before this, the young people attend Hebrew school with their rabbi to learn Hebrew, study the Torah, and prepare for their "calling up." Most parents throw elaborate parties after their children's bar and bat mitzvahs.

Jews have seven major annual festivals, although most non-religious Jews only observe Pesach (Passover) and Chanukah (Hanukkah). The Feast of Purim, held in March, remembers Queen Esther, the Jewish wife of a 4th-century Persian king, as told in the book of Esther in the Ketuvim. After the Persian Jews fasted for three days, she interceded with her husband to prevent wicked Haman's machinations to annihilate the Jews in the Persian Empire. Celebrating Purim involves reading the book of Esther at synagogue, and when Haman's name is mentioned, the children twirl graggers (noisemakers) or stamp their feet. Money or food is given to the poor, and people send gifts of food to their friends. The children and adults enjoy a feast and masquerade (demonstrating G-d's intervention behind the scenes).

Queen Esther reveals Haman's diabolical plot
Internet Archive Book Images, No restrictions, via Wikimedia Commons
https://commons.wikimedia.org/wiki/File:The_art_Bible,_comprising_the_Old_and_new_Testaments_-_with_numerous_illustrations_(1896)_(14780507284).jpg

Passover (Pesach) usually falls in April, celebrating G-d delivering the Israelites from enslavement in Egypt. On the first night of the week-long festival, families hold a seder: a special meal commemorating how G-d passed over each house with the lamb's blood on the door. The meal includes four glasses of wine, matzah bread, bitter herbs like horseradish that recall the harsh enslavement, and favorite dishes and delicacies.

A child asks, "Why is this night different from all other nights?" The foods are an object lesson teaching G-d's deliverance. Breaking the crisp matzah reminds the family of the Red Sea split open for the Israelites to walk across. The family thanks G-d for liberating their ancestors and prays for the Final Redemption when the Messiah comes. At the end of the meal, a cup of wine is poured, the door is opened, and the prophet Elijah is invited to join. Then everyone sings the Hallel, songs based on Moses and Miriam's song after crossing the Red Sea.

Shavuot (Pentecost or Feast of Weeks) is a two-day holiday in late May or early June celebrating G-d giving the Torah. Religious Jews observe this festival by reading the Torah all night, lighting candles, attending synagogue where the Ten Commandments are read, and enjoying a meal with dairy products. Shavuot is the festival the Jewish followers of Jesus were celebrating in Acts 2 of the New Testament.

Falling in September, Rosh Hashanah is the Jewish New Year, when Jews believe G-d created Adam and Eve. At the synagogue services, the shofar (ram's horn) is blown one hundred times to honor G-d as King of the Universe while the listeners contemplate how G-d fills all time and space. A wailing blow on the shofar reminds the congregation to reflect on their deeds and repent. The feast includes apples dipped in honey and challah bread with raisins to bring sweetness to the new year. Rosh Hashanah and Yom Kippur are the two Jewish high holidays.

Blowing the shofar near ancient Jerusalem's Western Wall
Amos Ben Gershom / Government Press Office, CC BY-SA 3.0 <https://creativecommons.org/licenses/by-sa/3.0>, via Wikimedia Commons; https://commons.wikimedia.org/wiki/File:Flickr_-_Government_Press_Office_(GPO)_-_The_Wailing_Wall_(cropped).jpg

Yom Kippur comes ten days after Rosh Hashanah and is the Day of Atonement, the holiest day of the Jewish year. G-d ordained this day in the Torah:

"And [all this] shall be as an eternal statute for you; in the seventh month, on the tenth of the month, you shall afflict yourselves, and you shall not do any work, neither the native nor the stranger who dwells among you. For on this day, He shall effect atonement for you to cleanse you. Before the L-rd, you shall be cleansed from all your sins. It is a Sabbath of rest for you, and you shall afflict yourselves. It is an eternal statute."[64]

Religious Jews "afflict" themselves by fasting from sunset until the following evening after the stars come out. They spend much of the time in introspection at the five services at synagogue, praying for forgiveness. The shofar is blown each morning for forty days before Yom Kippur, and Psalm 27 is recited: "Your presence, O L-rd, I will seek. Do not hide Your presence from me; do not turn Your servant away with anger. You were my help; do not forsake me and do not abandon me, O G-d of my salvation."[65]

Sukkot, or the Feast of Tabernacles, is a week-long holiday five days after Yom Kippur. It celebrates the harvest and G-d's protection of the Israelites when they left Egypt. Observant families erect outside booths covered with tree branches or palm fronds, where they eat their meals for the week. The booths remind them of the Israelites living in tents after leaving Egypt. The outdoor shelters also recall pilgrimages to Jerusalem and the temporary dwellings during the harvest. Each morning, the celebrants take a palm frond, a myrtle branch, a willow branch, and a citron, recite a blessing, and wave them while circling the synagogue.

Hanukkah (Chanukah) is the Festival of Lights celebrated eight days in December to remember the temple's rededication after the Maccabees drove the Greeks out of Judea. Antiochus Epiphanes IV had defiled the temple by sacrificing a pig to an idol of Saturn, and it needed to be purified. The lighting of the eight menorah candles in every household and synagogue reminds Jews of this time when evil forces were eradicated.

On the first night, one candle is lit after singing sacred blessings. On the second night, two are lit, and so on. A favorite food is latke (potato pancakes), and Jews in Israel love *sufganiyot* (jelly-filled doughnuts). Children have fun spinning the dreidel, a game using a four-sided top with Hebrew letters standing for an acrostic: "A great miracle happened there." Children receive gifts of money and give part of this to charity.

---

[64] Vayikra (Leviticus) 16:29-31

[65] Tehillim (Psalms) 27:7-9

The Star of David, two superimposed triangles, represents Judaism and Israel. In the 17th century, it marked Vienna's Jewish quarter and decorated synagogues. The Zionist movement used it in the 19th century, and the Nazis forced Jews to wear it on their clothing. Today, the blue Star of David is centered on Israel's white flag. The Jewish theologian Franz Rosenzweig proposed that the six points represent G-d, man, the world, creation, revelation, and redemption.

Star of David on Israel's flag
https://commons.wikimedia.org/wiki/File:Flag_of_Israel_(simplified).svg

Lions and eagles frequently decorate Torah scroll covers or the Torah Ark, where they are stored in the synagogue. The lions are usually next to a crown, representing Judah, the kingly tribe of David and the Messiah. The eagle represents G-d in the Song of Moses:

> "As an eagle awakens its nest, hovering over its fledglings, it spreads its wings, taking them and carrying them on its pinions, the L-rd guided them alone, and there was no alien deity with Him. He made them ride upon the high places of the earth."[66]

Jewish art includes elegant ceremonial objects, or Judaica, used in the synagogues and homes for Shabbat and sacred festivals. Some of these exquisite ritual objects are elaborate menorahs (candleholders), Torah covers, the fringed prayer shawl called a *tallit*, or the decorative pointer for reading the Torah called a *yad*. Another popular art form is Jewish papercuts with religious or mystical meanings that date back to the Middle Ages.

---

[66] Devarim (Deuteronomy) 32:11-13

This bowl fragment (300-350 CE) depicts a Torah Ark, menorah, and shofar.
Metropolitan Museum of Art, CC0, via Wikimedia Commons;
https://commons.wikimedia.org/wiki/File:Bowl_Fragments_with_Menorah,_Shofar,_and_Torah_Ark_MET_DP355178.jpg

Key Takeaways:

- ➤ Religion and customs
  - o Kosher: Devarim (Deuteronomy) 14:2-21 and Vayikra (Leviticus) 11
  - o Shabbat (Sabbath)
  - o Challah
  - o Bar and Bat Mitzvah
- ➤ Festivals
  - o Purim: Queen Esther defeats wicked Haman
  - o Passover (Pesach): deliverance from the angel of death and Egyptian slavery
  - o Shavuot/ Pentecost: celebrates G-d giving the Torah
  - o Rosh Hashanah: the Jewish New Year
  - o Yom Kippur: Day of Atonement
  - o Sukkot: Festival of Booths
  - o Hanukkah (Chanukah or Festival of Lights) celebrates the rededication of the temple

- Symbols
  - Star of David: represents Judaism and Israel
  - Lion of Judah
  - Eagle representing G-d from Song of Moses
- Art
  - Religious objects like menorahs and Torah covers
  - Papercuts

Chapter 10: Famous Jews: An Enthralling Collection

The rich and colorful history of Jewish people stretches back almost four thousand years. Some of the most well-known Jews not only contributed to their own culture but positively impacted the world through their faith, literature, scientific breakthroughs, and political acumen. Many suffered dreadfully in the Holocaust and other persecutions, yet their tenacity and courage continue to inspire.

Abraham (circa 20th century BCE)

Abraham was the great-grandfather of the twelve tribes of Israel. He grew up in Ur (in today's southern Iraq) during its third dynasty, the world's largest city of its day with a population of around 65,000. Ur-Nammu, who probably ruled during Abraham's lifetime, erected Ur's great ziggurat tower, built schools to teach cuneiform writing, and wrote the world's first known law code.

Following G-d's call, Abraham traveled to Canaan (today's Israel). G-d promised all the land of Canaan to Abraham's descendants: "And I will give you and your seed after you the land of your sojournings, the entire land of Canaan for an everlasting possession."[67]

Abraham's wife Sarah grew frustrated because she couldn't conceive, so she gave her Egyptian maidservant Hagar to Abraham as his wife.

---

[67] Bereshit (Genesis) 17:8

There was a custom that if a woman's maid became her husband's wife, the child born to the maid was considered the senior wife's child. Hagar gave birth to Ishmael, and the Torah says he settled in the northern Arabian Peninsula as an adult. Today's Muslims consider Ishmael a prophet and the ancestor of Muhammad.

G-d promised Abraham he would be the father of nations (plural). After Sarah died, Abraham married Keturah, and they had six sons: Zimran, Jokshan, Medan, Midian, Ishbak, and Shuah. The Jewish historian Josephus said that Zimran's descendants settled in Arabia, between Mecca and Medina, and Shuah's descendants lived in northern Syria on the Euphrates River. Jokshan's grandson Asshurim may have fathered the Semitic Assyrians of northern Iraq. Midian's descendants lived in northwestern Arabia; Moses's wife, Zipporah, was the daughter of Jethro, a Midianite priest.

Maimonides (1138-1204 CE)

Moshe (Moses) ben Maimon was born in Cordoba, Spain, at the end of the Jewish golden age under the rule of the Muslim taifa states. Descended from King David, he studied the Torah under his father, a judge. The Almohad Caliphate, a Berber Muslim dynasty, conquered Cordoba when Maimonides was around ten, forcing Jews and Christians to convert or leave. Maimonides's family went into exile, and he lived in southern Spain, Palestine, and North Africa for the next decade, studying medicine, philosophy, and Jewish law. He settled in Morocco, married, and had two sons. After relocating to Cairo, Egypt, he completed his commentary on the Mishna in 1168, a condensed overview of the Babylonian Talmud. His most outstanding work was the *Mishneh Torah*, the codification of Jewish law. He wrote *The Guide for the Perplexed*, attempting to reconcile Judaism with Aristotle's philosophy.

Another important work was his formulation of the thirteen fundamental beliefs of the Jewish faith. These core doctrines included the belief in one G-d, who was all-powerful and everywhere at once. Another essential belief was the resurrection from the dead when Moshiach (the Messiah) comes to renew and restore the Davidic dynasty. Maimonides upheld the unchanging teachings of the Torah given to Moses. He taught that those who follow the Torah receive an eternal reward, but the wicked are cut off from perpetual bliss.

While writing the *Mishneh Torah,* Maimonides served for about two years as the Nagid (prince) of the Jews in Egypt. Later, he was the court physician, Sultan Saladin's personal doctor. In addition to his works on theology and philosophy, Maimonides wrote medical treatises, including a guide on antidotes to various poisons and another guide on hygiene and a healthy lifestyle of moderation. He also wrote about conditions such as diabetes, pneumonia, asthma, and hepatitis and served as a physician to Jews, Muslims, and Christians.

Anne Frank (1929-45)

Anne Frank at her school in Amsterdam
https://commons.wikimedia.org/wiki/File:Anne_Frank_lacht_naar_de_schoolfotograaf.jpg

Born to Otto and Edith Frank in Frankfurt, Germany, Anne's Jewish family moved to Amsterdam to escape the rampant anti-Semitism and poor economic situation in Germany. Her father started a company selling spices and pectin, but when she was ten, Germany invaded Poland, beginning World War II. The following year, the Nazis conquered Holland.

When Anne was thirteen, her sixteen-year-old sister Margot received a notice telling her to report to a German labor camp, compelling her family to go into hiding immediately. Her father had been constructing a secret annex in the rear of the 300-year-old building housing his business. It was about 450 square feet on the second and third floors and could only be accessed by an entrance hidden by a revolving bookcase.

In July 1942, Anne and her family moved into the hidden apartment, joined by their neighbor Hermann van Pels, who had helped build the annex, and his wife and son. Her father's employees continued running the business in the front of the house and provided food and other essentials to the families in hiding. In November, a single man, Fritz Pfeffer, joined the two families in their tight secret quarters.

Just before going into hiding, Anne had received a diary for her thirteenth birthday. In her two years in the secret annex, she journaled about events, the people she lived with, and her fears and dreams. In August 1944, the police raided the building, discovered the secret hideout, and arrested Anne and the others. But after the police left, her father's employee found Anne's diary and kept it.

The Nazis transported Anne's family to the Auschwitz concentration camp in Poland. Three months later, they transferred the teenage Anne and Margot to the Bergen-Belsen concentration camp in Germany. The war was ending, but time was running out for Anne and Margot. Living in near-starvation conditions, they contracted typhus and died in February 1945, only three months before Germany surrendered.

Anne's father, Otto, was the only survivor of the eight people who had hidden in the secret annex. He returned to Amsterdam, where his former employee gave him Anne's diary. Moved by his adolescent daughter's account of life in hiding, he published it. The journal was eventually translated into seventy languages, and the secret annex became a museum. Anne's tragic story raised worldwide awareness of the Holocaust's horrors.

Albert Einstein (1879-1955)

Albert Einstein was born in Germany in 1879 to non-religious Jewish parents. He nurtured a curiosity about the Jewish faith as a child and supported the Zionist movement as an adult. Although unquestionably bright, Einstein did not speak in sentences until he was five. Disliking his German secondary school's rigid, pedantic teaching methods, he dropped out but later completed a Swiss secondary school. He graduated from the Swiss Federal Institute of Technology in Zurich despite frequently skipping classes.

In 1902, Einstein found employment in a Swiss patent office, examining patent applications in the mechanical field while pursuing doctoral studies at the University of Berlin. He described 1905 as his "annus mirabilis" (miracle year), publishing his treatise on the photoelectric effect, which won the Nobel Prize in 1920. In 1905, Einstein also published "On the Electrodynamics of Moving Bodies," the beginnings of his theory of relativity, which he completed in 1915. His formula $E=MC^2$ suggested that minuscule particles of matter could generate massive amounts of energy, paving the way for atomic power. His theory that mass causes space to curve was proven by measurements during the 1919 solar eclipse. Einstein continued to work at the patent office until receiving a professorship at the German University in Prague in 1911.

Albert Einstein
Comet Photo AG (Zürich), CC BY-SA 4.0 <https://creativecommons.org/licenses/by-sa/4.0>, via Wikimedia Commons; https://commons.wikimedia.org/wiki/File:Einstein_Com_M19-0053-0001.jpg

When Hitler became Germany's chancellor in 1933, the German press relentlessly attacked Einstein, and the Nazis publicly burned his scientific works and confiscated his bank accounts. He left for the United

States later that year, where he served at the Institute for Advanced Study in Princeton, New Jersey. He continued to work on quantum theory, the origins of the universe, and other pursuits until he died in 1955.

Although Einstein was not religious, he saw G-d in the harmony and precision of the universe, saying, "Everyone who is seriously involved in the pursuit of science becomes convinced that a spirit is manifest in the laws of the Universe—a spirit vastly superior to that of man, and one in the face of which we with our modest powers must feel humble."

Regarding his Jewish heritage, Einstein remarked, "The pursuit of knowledge for its own sake, an almost fanatical love of justice, and the desire for personal independence—these are the features of the Jewish tradition which make me thank my stars that I belong to."[68]

David Ben-Gurion: (1886-1973)

David Ben-Gurion was the primary founder of the modern State of Israel and its first prime minister. He was born David Yosef Gruen in 1886 in Plonsk, Poland, to a family committed to the Zionist movement. At age fourteen, he led a Zionist youth group where everyone spoke Hebrew. He immigrated to Palestine when he was twenty and quickly joined the Jewish Social Democratic Workers' Party, which aspired to the political independence of the Jews of Palestine. In 1909, he began writing for the party's newspaper *Ha'ahdut* and took the name Ben-Gurion.

After World War I broke out, the Ottoman Empire deported Ben-Gurion to Egypt in 1915 because of his Zionist activities. Shortly after, he left for a speaking tour in the United States, where he befriended influential Jewish-American leaders and met and married Paula Monbesz, a Russian-born fellow Zionist. The Ottoman Empire had ruled Palestine for four centuries, but in 1917, British troops captured Jerusalem. Ben-Gurion returned to Palestine and became the general secretary of the Zionist Labor Federation, rising to leadership of the Jews of Palestine.

When World War II began, Ben-Gurion advocated supporting the British war effort despite the 1939 White Paper declaring Britain's

---

[68]"Einstein's Deeply Held Political Beliefs," American Museum of Natural History. https://www.amnh.org/exhibitions/einstein/global-citizen#:~:text=Although%20Einstein%20did%20not%20observe,that%20I%20belong%20to%20it.%22

advocacy for a single Palestinian state with Arab majority rule. He also opposed the terrorist tactics of the Jewish underground freedom fighters. In 1942, he called for a swift founding of a Jewish state at the Zionist conference in New York. As the United Nations wrestled with the claims of Arabs and Jews to Palestine, Ben-Gurion began formulating plans for a democratic government.

On May 14, 1948, the People's Council declared the State of Israel and named Ben-Gurion its first prime minister and defense minister while people danced in the streets of Jerusalem. Following the War of Independence, Ben-Gurion developed the new state's institutions and managed the immigration of hundreds of thousands of Jews from Europe and Arab lands. He oversaw the building of new towns and cities around Israel.

Ben-Gurion retired from politics in 1953 to live on a kibbutz but returned to the position of defense minister in 1955 and was reelected as prime minister later that year. He spearheaded the 1956 invasion of the Sinai Peninsula and continued as prime minister until 1963. He again retired in 1970 and lived the rest of his life on a kibbutz in the Negev Desert, passing away in 1973.

Elie Wiesel (1928-2016)

Eliezer Wiesel was born to an Orthodox Jewish family in 1928 in Transylvania, Romania. In 1944, the German Nazis occupied his village, forcing the Jews to wear yellow stars and closing his parents' grocery store and other Jewish businesses. The family's Christian maid Maria begged them to come to her village in the mountains, where she had prepared a hideaway. Elie's father refused, unaware of the horrors that awaited them.

In early June 1944, when Elie was fifteen, the Nazis rounded up his family and forced them into a cattle car filled with eighty people. The train carried them to Auschwitz in Poland, where Elie and his father were camp laborers. The Nazis sent his mother and younger sister, Sarah, directly to the gas chambers. Elie and his father did not know whether his older sisters, Hilda and Bea, were dead or alive. In January 1945, the Nazis evacuated Auschwitz, forcing the inmates on a ten-day death march. Already starving, 14,000 prisoners died on the way.

The surviving six thousand prisoners were herded into freight cars and carried to Buchenwald concentration camp in Germany, but Elie's father died just after they arrived. In April, the guards began systematically shooting thousands of Jews and were preparing to evacuate the rest of the camp. However, as the Allied forces closed in, the Nazis fled, leaving the prisoners behind. US troops marched in on April 19, 1945, liberating the emaciated prisoners.

In this photo taken at Buchenwald Concentration Camp when the Allies arrived, Elie Wiesel is in the second row, the seventh prisoner from the left.
https://commons.wikimedia.org/wiki/File:Buchenwald_Slave_Laborers_Liberation.jpg

The Allies sent Elie and other underaged liberated prisoners to France. His older sisters had survived, and they all found each other two years later. Elie studied liberal arts at Sorbonne University but struggled with his faith, agonizing over G-d's seeming indifference to the suffering in the war. He found it cathartic to write down his experiences, and his book *Night* told of the horrors at Auschwitz and Buchenwald.

Elie wrote many more novels and memoirs along the same themes and became a human rights activist for Jews and other groups persecuted because of their race or religion. He advocated for the victims of South African apartheid and the Khmer Rouge atrocities in Cambodia. At President Carter's request, he led the United States Holocaust Memorial Council for six years. In 1986, he received the Nobel Peace Prize for his humanitarian efforts. He died in his home in Manhattan in 2016.

Benjamin Netanyahu (born 1949)

Benjamin (Bibi) Netanyahu is Israel's longest-serving prime minister, leading the nation for over fifteen years in three separate tenures. He was born in Tel Aviv in October 1949, three months after Israel won its War of Independence. His mother was born in Palestine, and his father was from Poland but immigrated to Palestine with his family when he was ten. Netanyahu spent most of his childhood in Jerusalem and part of his teen years in the United States when his father taught history at Dropsie College in Philadelphia.

Netanyahu returned to Israel at eighteen for his mandatory military service in Israel's Defense Forces (the IDF), fighting in its special forces. In the War of Attrition, he was shot in the shoulder during Operation Gift while freeing Jewish hostages from a hijacked airline in Beirut. He studied at MIT in Boston for his bachelor of science in architecture, returned to Israel to fight in the Yom Kippur War, then returned to MIT for his master of science in Management Studies.

Israel appointed Netanyahu as its ambassador to the United Nations in 1984. After serving four years, he returned to Israel and was elected to the Knesset from the right-wing Likud Party and appointed Deputy Minister of Foreign Affairs. He represented Israel in media interviews during the 1991 Gulf War.

Netanyahu won Israel's first direct elections for prime minister in 1996 and served until 1999. He became prime minister again in 2009, serving until 2021. Netanyahu clashed with US President Obama over his insistence that Israel stop building settlements in East Jerusalem and the West Bank. Netanyahu supported a demilitarized Palestinian state formed through direct negotiations between the Palestinians and Israel. He served in an interim capacity following the 2019 election debacle when neither party won a majority vote.

In March 2021, the fourth election in two years, Netanyahu's party won the most votes but not enough to form a government. His opponents formed a coalition government, ending Netanyahu's twelve-year tenure, but that government collapsed one year later. An increasing number of Israeli youths identified as right-wing, impacting Israel's political scene. By 2021, about 80 percent of Israel's population supported the right. In December 2022, Netanyahu was again sworn in as prime minister, with the most nationalistic and religiously conservative cabinet in Israel's history.

Key Takeaways:
- Abraham (circa 20th century BCE)
  - G-d promised Canaan (Israel) to his descendants as an eternal possession

- o Abraham fathered Ishmael, Isaac, Zimran, Jokshan, Medan, Midian, Ishbak, and Shuah. They settled in Canaan, northern Arabia, Syria, and east of Canaan.
➢ Maimonides (1138-1204 CE)
  - o Wrote a commentary on the Oral Torah, the Mishneh Torah, The Guide for the Perplexed, and Thirteen Principles of the Jewish Faith
  - o Served as the court physician and wrote medical treatises
➢ Anne Frank (1929-45)
  - o After the Nazis took Holland, her family hid in a secret annex for two years
  - o Eventually arrested and sent to a concentration camp, where she died
  - o Her father published her diary, raising awareness of the Holocaust
➢ Albert Einstein (1879-1955)
  - o Developed the theory of relativity
  - o Received a Nobel Prize for his treatise on the photoelectric effect in 1930
  - o Believed G-d could be seen in the laws of the universe
➢ David Ben-Gurion: (1886-1973)
  - o Avid Zionist who led Jews in Palestine before independence
  - o Became the first prime minister of the new State of Israel and minister of defense
➢ Elie Wiesel (1928-2016)
  - o Teen survivor of Auschwitz and Buchenwald concentration camps
  - o Author and humanitarian activist for oppressed people
  - o Received Nobel Peace Prize in 1986
➢ Benjamin Netanyahu (born 1949)
  - o Born in Tel Aviv, raised in Jerusalem and the United States
  - o Israel's longest-serving prime minister: over fifteen years in three separate tenures

Conclusion

Judaism and the Jewish people have radically impacted world history for thousands of years. With their stellar contribution to the sciences, humanities, and economics, Jews continue to play an illustrious role on the world stage.

Judaism gave birth to Christianity, the world's largest religion today. Jesus and his initial group of disciples were all Jewish, and they continued to worship in Jerusalem's temple, attend synagogue throughout the Jewish diaspora, and observe the traditional feasts. Jesus explicitly supported the entire Tanakh: "Don't think that I came to destroy the law or the prophets. I didn't come to destroy, but to fulfill."[69]

The Apostle Paul, who studied under Gamaliel the Elder, built his teachings around the Tanakh. The Jewish writers of the New Testament quoted directly from the Tanakh 283 times and referred to it over 1,000 times. The Christian Church adopted the entire Tanakh into the biblical canon. Christianity initially spread through the Jewish diaspora communities around the Mediterranean.

Judaism also heavily impacted Islam, the world's second-largest religion, which adopted the belief in one G-d. Muslims believe Abraham, Ishmael, Moses, Job, Joseph, and David were prophets who brought divine revelation. The Quran refers to Adam's creation, Noah and the flood, Abraham's covenant, and Moses receiving God's revelation on Mount Sinai. Christianity and Islam also follow Judaism's

---

[69] Matthew 5:17, *World English Bible*.

teaching of Shabbat, or a day of rest (although in Christianity it is Sunday, and in Islam it is Friday).

In modern history, Jews have been incredibly successful. The Nobel Prizes recognize the Jewish contributions to medicine, the sciences, literature, economics, and peace: despite comprising less than 1 percent of the world's population, 22 percent of Nobel laureates have been Jews.

In medicine, Gertrude Elion developed a treatment for childhood leukemia, and Bruce Beutler continues his brilliant research in immunity and inflammation. Ralph Steinman discovered dendritic cells and launched the first clinical trial of a cell-targeted HIV vaccine. Paul Ehrlich discovered a cure for syphilis, and Rosalind Franklin pioneered work on the molecular structure of viruses and DNA. Otto Loewi's research demonstrated that chemicals relay nerve signals to organs. The neurobiologist Rita Levi-Montalcini discovered nerve growth factor. Albert Einstein, Niels Bohr, Wolfgang Pauli, and John von Neumann (a genius savant) made staggering contributions to mathematics, physics, economics, and computer science. Alexandre Friedmann developed the Big Bang Theory. Claude Levi-Strauss made strides in structural anthropology and sociology.

In technology, Siegfried Marcus made the first gasoline-fueled vehicle in 1864, and Paul Zoll developed the cardiac pacemaker and defibrillator. Gordon Gould invented the laser, and Isidor Isaac Rabi developed nuclear magnetic resonance used in MRIs. Zhores Alferov developed semiconductor heterostructures and furthered technology in solar cells and LEDs. Israeli entrepreneur Dov Moran invented the USB memory stick. Bob Kahn gave us the internet by developing IP (Internet Protocol) and TCP (Transmission Control Protocol) that empower communication between computers. Mark Zuckerberg, Dustin Moskovitz, and Eduardo Saverin invented Facebook in a Harvard dorm room.

In commerce, Levi Strauss, a Bavarian immigrant to San Francisco, invented blue jeans in the 1880s to meet the needs of miners in the gold rush. Jewish entrepreneur Emil Jellinek financed the development of the Daimler-Mercedes (later Mercedes-Benz), the fastest car in the races in Nice, France. Charles Lazarus founded Toys "R" Us in 1959. Jewish fashion and cosmetic enterprises include Calvin Klein, Donna Karan, Estée Lauder, Fabergé, Gap, Max Factor, Ralph Lauren, and Revlon. In the food and beverage industry, Howard Schultz launched Starbucks.

Reuben and Rose Mattus invented Häagen-Dazs ice cream, giving it a Danish-sounding name because of the Danes' kind treatment of Jews in World War II. Entrepreneur William Rosenberg founded Dunkin' Donuts.

Paul Rosenberg and Solomon Guggenheim furthered the world art market with their art collections, the Guggenheim Museum, and Rosenberg's financial assistance to Picasso. Paul Rosenberg and his wife fled France in 1940 when the Nazis invaded, leaving behind two thousand priceless pieces, which the Nazis sent to Germany. He was able to reclaim or repurchase some of the art after the war. Paul's brother Léonce, also an art collector and dealer, stayed in France but went into hiding and lost his entire inventory.

Authors such as science fiction writer Isaac Asimov and novelists Franz Kafka and Marcel Proust have graced the world of modern literature. Film directors like Steven Spielberg and Woody Allen have captured the imaginations of millions of viewers. Felix Mendelssohn's compositions, Johann Strauss's waltzes, and Leonard Bernstein's conducting have left a mark on classical music.

Well-known Jewish pop music artists include Neil Diamond and his high school classmate Barbra Streisand, who sang together in their school's choral club. Another Jewish classmate at their Erasmus Hall High School in Brooklyn was Bobby Fischer, the world chess champion. (Half of the world's top chess grandmasters between 1851 and 2000 were Jews.) Simon Garfunkel was a cantor in his synagogue and met his future music partner Paul Simon (also a Jew) in sixth grade in Queens. Bob Dylan was originally Robert Zimmerman from a Russian Jewish family who settled in Minnesota. Billy Joel's Jewish father, a classical pianist, escaped the Nazi regime in Germany as a child.

Today, the world's Jewish population is 15.3 million, with about 7 million living in Israel, 6 million in the United States, and the rest in France, Canada, the United Kingdom, or scattered over the globe. Despite staggering odds, the modern State of Israel was born three years after the end of the "Shoah" (Holocaust). Its neighbors vowed to wipe it off the Middle Eastern map, but Israel's military prowess and political acumen held strong.

Yet Israel hasn't only survived. It has thrived economically as the world's "start-up nation," with more new businesses per capita than any other country. Its per capita Gross Domestic Product is in the top twenty in the world, ahead of much of Europe, Japan, and Canada. It is a beacon of prosperity, utilizes world-class technology, and has a vibrant, albeit contentious, democracy. Around the world, Jewish history has revealed a people who are indomitable high achievers, skilled in adapting to innumerable challenges.

Here's another book by Enthralling History that you might like

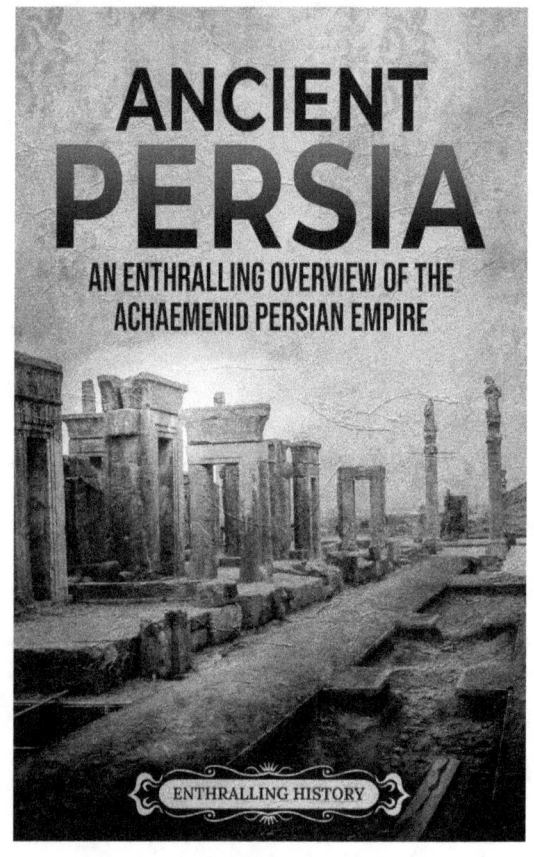

Free limited time bonus

Stop for a moment. We have a free bonus set up for you. The problem is this: we forget 90% of everything that we read after 7 days. Crazy fact, right? Here's the solution: we've created a printable, 1-page pdf summary for this book that you're reading now. All you have to do to get your free pdf summary is to go to the following website:

https://livetolearn.lpages.co/enthrallinghistory/

Once you do, it will be intuitive. Enjoy, and thank you!

Bibliography

Alstola, Tero. "Judean Merchants in Babylonia and Their Participation in Long-Distance Trade." *Die Welt Des Orients* 47, no. 1 (2017): 25-51. http://www.jstor.org/stable/26384887.

Baker, Luke. "Ancient Tablets Reveal Life of Jews in Nebuchadnezzar's Babylon." *Reuters*,

Bareket, Elinoar. "The Head of the Jews (Ra'is al-Yahud) in Fatimid Egypt: A Re-Evaluation." *Bulletin of the School of Oriental and African Studies, University of London* 67, no. 2 (2004): 185-97. http://www.jstor.org/stable/4145978.

Baron, Salo W. *A Social and Religious History of the Jews.* New York: Columbia University Press, 1957.

Baskin, Judith R. ed. and Kenneth Seeskin, ed. *The Cambridge Guide to Jewish History, Religion, and Culture.* New York: Cambridge University Press, 2012.

Bertman, Stephen. *Handbook to Life in Ancient Mesopotamia.* Oxford: Oxford University Press, 2005.

Brenner, Michael. *After the Holocaust: Rebuilding Jewish Lives in Postwar Germany.* Translated by Barbara Harshav. Princeton: Princeton University Press, 1997.

Brook, Kevin Alan. *The Jews of Khazaria.* Lanham, Maryland: Rowman & Littlefield, 2018.

Cohen, Mark R. "Jews in the Mamlūk Environment: The Crisis of 1442 (A Geniza Study)." *Bulletin of the School of Oriental and African Studies, University of London* 47, no. 3 (1984): 425-48. http://www.jstor.org/stable/618879.

Cohn-Sherbok, Dan. *Judaism: History, Belief and Practice.* New York: Routledge, 2017.

Cohn-Wein, Eli. *The Golden Age of Jewish Philosophy.* Sefaria. https://www.sefaria.org/sheets/327268?lang=bi

Dalley, Stephanie. Myths from Mesopotamia Creation, the Flood, Gilgamesh, and Others. Oxford: Oxford University Press, 2008.

Delorme, Jean-Philippe. "בת דוד in the Mesha Stele: A Defense of André Lemaire's Reading and Its Historical Implications." *SBL and AAR New England and Eastern Canada Region Annual Meeting.* Tufts University, Massachusetts, March 22, 2019.

"Einstein's Deeply Held Political Beliefs." *American Museum of Natural History.* https://www.amnh.org/exhibitions/einstein/global-citizen#:~:text=Although%20Einstein%20did%20not%20observe,that%20I%20belong%20to%20it.%22

Enuma Elish: The Seven Tablets of Creation. Translated by Leonard William King. London: Luzac, 1902. https://www.sacred-texts.com/ane/enuma.htm

Eridu Genesis. Translated by Thorkild Jacobson. Livius, accessed October 18, 2021. https://www.livius.org/sources/content/oriental-varia/eridu-genesis/

Gibb, H. A. R. The Damascus Chronicle of the Crusades: Extracted and Translated from the Chronicle of Ibn Al-Qalanisi. Mineola, New York: Dover Publications, 2003.

Haas, Richard N. "Israel at 75." *The Strategist: Australian Strategic Policy Institute.* May 23, 2023. https://www.aspistrategist.org.au/israel-at-75/

Herodotus. *Capture of Babylon.* Livius. https://www.livius.org/articles/person/darius-the-great/sources/capture-of-babylon-herodotus/

"Immigration to Israel: The First Aliyah (1882-1903)." *Jewish Virtual Library.*

Jacob, Walter, ed. The Pittsburgh Platform in Retrospect: The Changing World of Reform Judaism. Pittsburgh: Rodef Shalom Congregation Press, 1985.

Johnson, Paul. *A History of the Jews.* New York: Harper & Row, 1987.

Josephus, Flavius. *The Antiquities of the Jews.* Translated by William Whiston. Project Gutenberg EBook. https://www.gutenberg.org/files/2848/2848-h/2848-h.htm

Josephus, Flavius. *The Wars of the Jews.* Translated by William Whiston. Project Gutenberg EBook. https://www.gutenberg.org/files/2850/2850-h/2850-h.htm

Lenin, Theodore I., et al. *Associates, Rabbi and Synagogue in Reform Judaism.* West Harford: Central Conference of American Rabbis, 1972, 98-99.

Marcus, Jacob. *The Jew in the Medieval World: A Sourcebook, 315-1791.* New York: Jewish Publication Society, 1938.

Meyer, Michael A. Response to Modernity: A History of the Reform Movement in Judaism. New York: Oxford University Press, 1988.

Minsky, Michael G. *Agobard and His Relations with the Jews.* Amherst: University of Massachusetts, 1971.

Na'aman, Nadav. "Three Notes on the Aramaic Inscription from Tel Dan." *Israel Exploration Journal* 50, no. ½ (2000): 92-104. http://www.jstor.org/stable/27926919.

Nebel, Almut, Dvora Filon, Deborah A. Weiss, Michael Weale, Marina Faerman, Ariella Oppenheim, Mark G. Thomas. "High-resolution Y Chromosome Haplotypes of Israeli and Palestinian Arabs Reveal Geographic Substructure and Substantial Overlap with Haplotypes of Jews." *Human Genetics.* 107, no. 6 (December 2000): 630-641. doi:10.1007/s004390000426.

Pollock, Susan. *Ancient Mesopotamia.* Cambridge: Cambridge University Press, 1999.

Rohl, John C. G. The Kaiser and His Court: Wilhelm II and the Government of Germany. Cambridge: Cambridge University Press, 1995.

"S/Agenda/58." *Security Council Official Records.* (April 16, 1948), 19.

Shagrir, Iris, and Netta Amir. "The Persecution of the Jews in the First Crusade: Liturgy, Memory, and Nineteenth-Century Visual Culture." *Speculum* 92, no. 2 (2017): 405-28. http://www.jstor.org/stable/26340194.

Shaus, Arie, Yana Gerber, Shira Faigenbaum-Golovin, Barak Sober, Eli Piasetzky, and Israel Finkelstein. "Forensic Document Examination and Algorithmic Handwriting Analysis of Judahite Biblical Period Inscriptions Reveal Significant Literacy Level." *PLOS One.* September 9, 2020. https://doi.org/10.1371/journal.pone.0237962 S

Stub, Sara Toth. "Letter from Ethiopia: Exploring a Forgotten Jewish Land." *Archaeology.* January/February 2023. https://www.archaeology.org/issues/498-2301/letter-from/11057-ethiopia-beta-israel

Talmud. The William Davidson Edition. Sefaria. https://www.sefaria.org/texts/Talmud

The Book of Maccabees II. Second Temple. Sefaria. https://www.sefaria.org/The_Book_of_Maccabees_II?tab=contents

"The Code of Hammurabi." Translated by L.W. King. In *The Avalon Project: Documents in Law, History, and Diplomacy.* Yale Law School: Lillian Goldman Law Library. https://avalon.law.yale.edu/ancient/hamframe.asp

The Complete Tanakh: The Jewish Bible with a Modern English Translation and Rashi's Commentary.

https://www.chabad.org/library/bible_cdo/aid/63255/jewish/The-Bible-with-Rashi.htm

"The Program of the National-Socialist German Workers' Party, February 24, 1920." *Jewish Virtual Library.* https://www.jewishvirtuallibrary.org/platform-of-the-national-socialist-german-workers-rsquo-party

"The Question of Palestine." *United Nations.* https://www.un.org/unispal/history/#:~:text=After%20looking%20at%20alternatives%2C%20the,(II)%20of%201947).

"The Suez Crisis, 1956." *Office of the Historian.* Foreign Service Institute: United States Department of State. https://history.state.gov/milestones/1953-1960/suez#:~:text=On%20July%2026%2C%201956%2C%20Egyptian,since%20its%20construction%20in%201869.

Van De Mieroop, Marc. *A History of the Ancient Near East ca. 3000 - 323 BC.* Hoboken: Blackwell Publishing, 2006.

Van Maaren, John. *The Boundaries of Jewishness in the Southern Levant 200 BCE–132 CE.* 43-108. Boston: De Gruyter, 2022. https://doi.org/10.1515/9783110787450-002

www.ingramcontent.com/pod-product-compliance
Lightning Source LLC
Chambersburg PA
CBHW070336010526
44107CB00004B/530